Praise for *Called to Christian Joy and Maturity*

"Only a mature missionary disciple will be able to weather the storms of the world we live in today and discern how the Holy Spirit is leading them to serve the New Evangelization. With this unique focus on Christian maturity, Gordy DeMarais and Dan Keating share their experie~ ~ipleship with young adults gained over m~ s. Having been formed myself i~ ching as a member of Saint I lege, I highly recommend thi ...o help other young people reach the fu ...rist desires for them."
—**The Most Rev. Andre\ ~zzens, STD, DD, Chairman of the Committee on Evangelization and Catechesis, United States Conference of Catholic Bishops**

"What a blessing it is that DeMarais and Keating continue to take up the mantle of missionary discipleship. *Called to Christian Joy and Maturity* is a valuable instruction for those wanting to see the seed of conversion mature into a Christian person overflowing with joy and capable to making missionary disciples."
—**Curtis Martin, Founder, Fellowship of Catholic University Students (FOCUS)**

"Gordon DeMarais and Daniel Keating have written a very important book for our times. It is becoming more important than ever that communities of mature missionary disciples are formed for the Church. DeMarais and Keating bring a fresh and experienced outlook to community-based discipleship. We can see at Benedictine College the impact that Saint Paul's Outreach and its commitment to community-based discipleship has had on our students. This book takes that knowledge and expands it for the greater good of the Church."

—**Stephen Minnis, President, Benedictine College**

"The Catholic Church is blessed—she is holy, the Body of Christ, and a beautiful bride worthy of all our efforts to fight for her. She is also tattered, torn, and beaten up. And we, the members of the Church, are the cause of this—rather than fighting for her we have abandoned her and fought against her. I can't think of an ill plaguing the Church that wouldn't immediately be made better if we were faithful, missionary disciples. At the heart of most, if not all, of our problems is we the body of Christ have failed to be disciples of Jesus who long for holiness, transformation, and a zeal to bring others to him.

In their book, *Called to Christian Joy and Maturity*, Gordon DeMarais and Daniel Keating do a wonderful job at presenting the tremendous need we have for men and women to take up the invitation to be disciples. In a way that is eminently accessible they offer a path to discipleship that is practical, inspirational, and effective. In the end, the reader will be left with the belief that being a faithful disciple of Jesus is not only possible, but the only way a Christian ought to live."

—**Fr. Dave Pivonka, TOR, President, Franciscan University of Steubenville**

"*Called to Christian Joy and Maturity* is an excellent resource which will be a sure help in implementing the New Evangelization. Keating and DeMarais demonstrate the vital mission we have of helping people come to Christian maturity after they have had an initial encounter with Christ. Their years of experience in forming Catholic disciples provide critical insights for priests, parish staffs, and any intentional disciple who wants to help people grow in their faith.

This book will help anyone who engages it seriously to be a better witness to the gospel, a more confident mentor, and have a clearer strategic plan for helping others go from a desire to follow Christ to becoming a mature and joyful disciple of Jesus Christ."
—Fr. Stephen Pullis, Director of Evangelization and Missionary Discipleship, Archdiocese of Detroit

"It's so vital to integrate the task of evangelization and the work of our own conversion, and this book teaches us—with intellectual rigor and practical insight—how to be both "missionary" and "disciple." For a culture burdened by fear and boredom, these words are an encouragement, a challenge, and a gift. What an inspiration to embrace with ever more courage and zeal the great adventure of life with Jesus Christ!"
—Msgr. James Shea, President, University of Mary

Called to Christian Joy and Maturity

FORMING MISSIONARY DISCIPLES

Gordon C. DeMarais
Daniel A. Keating

the WORD among us® press

Published by The Word Among Us Press
7115 Guilford Drive, Suite 100
Frederick, Maryland 21704
wau.org

25 24 23 22 21   1 2 3 4 5

ISBN: 978-1-59325-387-5
eISBN: 978-1-59325-388-2

Design by Suzanne Earl

Made and printed in the United States of America

Library of Congress Control Number: 2021908092

CONTENTS

Acknowledgments

We would like to thank Jeff Smith, who when he overheard we were hoping to co-author a book on forming missionary disciples, immediately offered to have The Word Among Us publish the book. We are grateful to Beth McNamara who has worked with us from the beginning to coax the book into existence and guide it to completion. We are also thankful for the excellent editing skills of Cynthia Cavnar, Jessica Montgomery, and Lucy Scholand, who took an awkward manuscript and shaped it into a much better and clearer book.

Preface

In his apostolic exhortation *Evangelii Gaudium*, Pope Francis calls all Christians to embrace the call to become missionary disciples:

> The Church which "goes forth" is a community of missionary disciples who take the first step, who are involved and supportive, who bear fruit and rejoice. An evangelizing community knows that the Lord has taken the initiative, he has loved us first (cf. 1 Jn 4:19), and therefore we can move forward, boldly take the initiative, go out to others, seek those who have fallen away, stand at the crossroads and welcome the outcast.[1]

Likewise, George Weigel speaks about the need to form communities of missionary disciples as our best strategy for the Church today. To evangelize the postmodern world of the twenty-first century, Weigel believes, we need to be grounded in the Gospel truth, "a truth that forms a mission-centered community of disciples with a clear sense of identity and purpose."[2] The result will be "a culture-forming counterculture for the sake of the world, its healing, and its conversion."[3]

We offer this book in the hope of making a contribution to the wide-ranging efforts being made today to equip the Church to become a joyful band, a community, of missionary disciples.

Many are laboring in this field and bearing a rich harvest. In July 2017, the United States Conference of Catholic Bishops held a convocation for several thousand Catholic leaders in Orlando, Florida, entitled "The Joy of the Gospel in America." Leaders gathered to listen, share, pray, and engage in a strategic conversation about how to form missionary disciples who will animate the Church and engage the surrounding culture. This unprecedented gathering, which continued for four days, had a single aim: that the Church might be better equipped to form missionary disciples who will effectively bring Christ to the world.

We write this book with deep appreciation for what we have learned from many authors who have shaped our understanding of the task we face. Sherry Weddell's groundbreaking book, *Forming Intentional Disciples*, has helped create a category for intentional discipleship in the Church today.[4]

Many people in the Church first learned what discipleship is by encountering Weddell's vibrant presentation. Our book is intended to complement what Weddell has laid down as a foundation. Her book is especially focused on conversion and the initial decision to intentionally follow Christ as his disciples. Our treatment includes the stage of conversion but focuses on what happens after this: how can we help people move from the initial decision to become disciples through a *process* of formation that leads to *maturity* in discipleship?

Curtis Martin, the founder of FOCUS, has contributed an inspiring volume called *Making Missionary Disciples*.[5] Basing his book on the pattern laid down in the Gospels, Martin shows the importance of creating a culture in which missionary disciples can live, grow, and develop key habits that enable them to be fruitful throughout their lives. Our book builds on these foundations and explores what it means for people to grow to maturity as missionary disciples within a community—a culture—that is conducive to forming new disciples in Christ.[6]

This book is a fruit of our nearly four decades of experience in forming mature missionary disciples of Christ. We have worked most often with young adults, from late high school through university and into early adulthood. But we have also helped men and women in many stages of life follow the call of discipleship.

Gordy DeMarais is the founder and president of St. Paul's Outreach, a Catholic student outreach located on campuses in North America.[7] Daniel Keating, a professor of theology at Sacred Heart Major Seminary (Detroit, Michigan), served for twenty-five years with University Christian Outreach, an ecumenical student ministry located in North America and abroad.[8]

We have weathered many ups and downs in ministry: we have known the gratifying experience of seeing many young people respond to the call of God and become disciples of Christ; we have also known failure and made wrong turns in ministry. We remain committed to the crucial task of forming mature missionary disciples in and for the Church today.

This book consists of six chapters. In chapter 1, we ask the question "Why Discipleship?" Why is the strategy of forming mature missionary disciples, in the context of community, so central to the task of the New Evangelization today?

In the second chapter, "Biblical Patterns of Discipleship," we turn to the example of Jesus himself: how did Christ go about calling and forming disciples to share in his work? We are not seeking a strict blueprint in the Gospels but rather patterns of discipleship that can guide our efforts today.

In chapter 3, "Discipleship Is a Process," we present a central principle of disciple making: forming disciples involves a process that occurs in recognizable stages over time. Our goal is to describe these stages and how we help people move from stage to stage.

In chapter 4, "Vehicles of Formation," we ask, "What are the key *vehicles*, or carriers, that assist the process of disciple making?" The temptation is to rely on one approach. Our experience shows that several vehicles, working together, provide the best context for helping people grow into dedicated, balanced, and mature disciples of Christ.

In the fifth chapter, "Characteristics of a Mature Missionary Disciple," we consider the primary traits that should be evident in a mature disciple as results of discipleship formation. In the final chapter, "A Lifelong Vision for Adventurous Discipleship," we turn to the costly, adventurous aspect of following Christ. What does it mean to be a witness to Christ, and how can we embrace the unpredictable, challenging aspects of discipleship? Here we point to the centrality of faith, hope, and love for lifelong discipleship and show the blessing of godly friendship as we seek to become—and to live as—a joyful band of missionary disciples of Jesus Christ.

Our prayer is that this book will contribute to the task of forming communities of mature missionary disciples in and for the Church today. All for the glory of God!

CHAPTER 1

Why Discipleship?

The goal of this chapter is to situate the call to mature Christian discipleship within the current state of our world and to show that, because of the times we live in, the priority for the Church today includes both a New Evangelization and the formation of mature Christian disciples.

Inspired by no earthly ambition, the Church seeks but a solitary goal: to carry forward the work of Christ under the lead of the befriending Spirit. . . .

To carry out such a task, the Church has always had the duty of scrutinizing the signs of the times and of interpreting them in the light of the Gospel. Thus, in language intelligible to each generation, she can respond to the perennial questions which men ask about this present life and the life to come, and about the relationship of the one to the other. We must therefore recognize and understand the world in which we live, its explanations, its longings, and its often dramatic characteristics. . . .

Today, the human race is involved in a new stage of history.[9]

My wife and I (Gordy) had finally completed our evening parenting duties. Our (then four) children were down for the night, or so we thought. I was working in my office when my oldest son, Peter, who was ten years old at the time, walked through the door.

"So we get up every morning, get dressed, go to school or work, come home, eat dinner, go to sleep?" he asked. "And then we do that day after day until one day we die?"

"Yep, Son, that's about right," I responded without looking up and then went back to the mountain of bills I was working through.

"I don't get it," he said. I stopped what I was doing and looked up at him. I knew this was an important moment.

"Not getting it" is a first step toward faith. I began to recall the moments in my life when I didn't get it. The first was when I was fifteen, and I remember it vividly. It was a few days after I had finished my freshman year in high school. My mom called home that evening around six o'clock and said she wouldn't be home for dinner. She was at the hospital, where she had spent a good deal of her time over the previous months with my father, who at the age of forty-three was battling cancer that had robbed him of his job, his hair, half his weight, and virtually every comforting activity this passing world can offer. And now this cancer was aiming to take the life that remained.

At about 2:00 a.m., my grandmother woke me up. I can still picture the moment. I was coming out of sleep on the top bunk of a bed my brother and I shared. I heard my grandmother say, "Wake up, Rusty (my nickname)! Your father has passed away." At 3:00 a.m. I sat at the kitchen table with my mother, my brother who was a year younger, and my grandparents. My five other siblings, all younger, were still asleep.

My world was shattered. It was as if a veil was ripped from my soul; the emptiness was unbearable. The days that followed still sit in my memory. I didn't get it. The deepest part of me was raw and exposed.

That time remains a watershed experience in my life. I was confronting life's ultimate questions: How can we make sense of suffering, injustice, and death? What is the meaning of life? Who am I? Where did I come from? Unless we can make sense of these questions, we cannot make sense of life. This is the beginning of faith.

At the beginning of Jesus' public ministry, we find him off alone, in prayer, after preaching to the crowds gathered at the home of Simon Peter's mother-in-law. "Simon and those who were with him followed him, and they found him and said to him, 'Everyone is searching for you'" (Mark 1:36-37).

> In Jesus Christ and through his death and resurrection, we are freed from slavery to sin and death and become new creations who can share in the life of God for eternity.

Every human person is searching for God. This thirst for God, though often not explicitly acknowledged, is manifest in our deepest longings and our search for the ultimate meaning of our lives and of the world. This search is an authentic preamble to the faith because it can guide people onto the path that leads to God.

It is our conviction that in Jesus Christ alone we find the compelling response to these questions that reside in every human heart. The good news is that in Jesus Christ and through his death and resurrection, we are freed from slavery to sin and death and become new creations who can share in the life of God for eternity. This gospel does not change. It transcends history, time, and culture. It is also the case that this good news was proclaimed to people who lived in a particular moment in history, in a particular place and culture, as recorded in the Bible. This historical and cultural context, so different from our own, presents us with the urgent need to consider the gospel from the perspective of our own times if we are to proclaim the good news of Jesus Christ and live according to the gospel.

Without question, we are experiencing in our day a faith crisis of immense proportion. The bishops who gathered for the Second Vatican Council recognized this: "Today, the human race is involved in a new stage of history."[10]

Pope St. John Paul II, in his apostolic exhortation *Christifidelis Laici* [On the Role of the Laity in the Church], says something similar. He describes "a new state of affairs today both in the Church and in social, economic, political and cultural life" that "calls with a particular urgency" for the active participation of all followers of Christ to labor in the Lord's vineyard.[11]

In this first chapter, we will consider the nature of these challenges and why our current situation requires a new evangelization that makes forming mature missionary disciples a priority.

The Signs of the Times

Upon graduating from the College of St. Thomas in St. Paul, Minnesota, I (Gordy) accepted a job leading evangelistic retreats for junior and senior high school students at the St. Paul Catholic Youth Center, an archdiocesan ministry. My family didn't quite understand my career path and weren't overly enthusiastic in their support. They were happy to see me turn my life around and return to the Church, but the idea that a layperson would work full-time in Church ministry was foreign to them.

My grandfather approached me at a family gathering and stuck a five-dollar bill in my pocket. "Gordy, I am not quite sure what you are doing with your life," he said. "I was going to give this money to the missions, but somehow I figure giving it to you is the same thing."

My grandparents were faithful Catholics, exemplary in many ways, but they lived in a world very different from today's. They lived in a time when the practice of faith was a given, and being an agnostic or atheist was rare. Faith was effectively passed from generation to generation, and young people lived in a culture that called them out of their own self-preoccupation to a greatness expressed in living sacrificially and in service of others, for the common good. That day is not today.

In my early years of evangelizing and forming young adults, I kept a file that I called "The Signs of the Times." When I came across news clippings, journal articles, or surveys that highlighted troubling trends emerging in the culture and in the Church, I put them in that file, and then I used them in my speaking and writing. I stopped that practice some years ago, when I realized that nearly every report I came across was troubling.

One of the "Signs of the Times" is the increasing number of "nones." Nones are those who claim no religious affiliation. They include atheists, agnostics, and those who are "nothing in particular."

A recent survey from Pew Research confirms that the decline of Christianity in the United States is continuing at a rapid pace. From 2009 to 2019, the percentage of nones in the overall adult population in the US grew from 17 percent to 26 percent. Among young adults, the percentage of nones rose astonishingly, from 25 percent to 40 percent. In that same ten-year span in the United States, the percentage of adults who identify as Catholic decreased from 23 percent to 20 percent of the population. This means that in the US there are more people who claim to have no religious affiliation than there are those who claim to be Catholic.[12]

On October 11, 2012, Pope Benedict proclaimed a Year of Faith. He called the Church to a renewal of faith because he recognized the continuing and rapid decline of Christianity in places where it was once foundational, especially in Europe and the United States. It is a mistake, he suggested, for us to continue "to think of the faith as a self-evident presupposition for life in society. In reality, not only can this presupposition no longer be taken for granted, but it is often openly denied." He recognized "a profound crisis of faith that has affected many people."[13] For his part, St. John Paul II said,

> Whole countries and nations where religion and the Christian life were formerly flourishing and capable of fostering a viable and working community of faith are now put to a hard test and, in some cases, are even undergoing a radical transformation, as a result of a constant spreading of an indifference to religion, of secularism and atheism.[14]

What has emerged is what Pope St. John Paul II called a culture of death. It is a culture that has forgotten God,[15] that lives "as if God did not exist."[16]

When a society rejects God as its foundational principle, humanity then asserts itself in place of God. This is, of course, not a new temptation but in fact the original sin.

Radical selfishness is at the core of the culture of death. In this culture of consumerism and hedonism, men and women pursue pleasure, power, and possessions for their own sake, and they treat people as things to be discarded when they are no longer useful. Pope Francis calls this our "throwaway culture" and notes that it impacts the entire planet.[17] Within this culture of materialism, humanity denies spiritual realities or considers them insignificant. In short, God is irrelevant.

The crisis of faith has particular consequences for young people and future generations. I (Gordy) sit on the advisory board of the United States Conference of Catholic

Bishops (USCCB) Committee on Campus Ministry. A couple of years ago, we conducted a study that surveyed the landscape of Catholic campus ministry across the country.[18] The study affirmed the crisis of Catholic life and faith on college campuses. On average, 9.7 percent of Catholic students on college campuses are attending Mass regularly ("regularly" defined as once a month). That means over 90 percent are not. Only 4.1 percent participate in some kind of spiritual activity outside of Sunday Mass; that means over 95 percent do not. A mere 1.7 percent frequent the Sacrament of Reconciliation.

Campus ministers described the campus culture as "hostile to maintaining Catholic faith." There were many comments like "It is a challenge for students to live their faith on a campus where religion is not common and even ostracized both by their peers and in the classroom," "Students are challenged regularly to a disintegrating and diminishing view of the human person and the widespread acceptance of sexual immorality," and "Party and hookup culture characterize the social environment."

Many students who were active in their faith reported significant challenges: loneliness, anxiety, addiction to media and gaming, sexual immorality and pornography, and hopelessness about the future, to mention a few. Our young people are losing their faith and abandoning sexual morality in college, and most are not returning to the faith later in life.

I spoke with Fr. Philip Merdinger, who formerly served as the national chaplain for Saint Paul's Outreach (SPO). Fr. Philip is eighty years old, has founded a religious order, and spent most of his priestly ministry on college campuses, working with university students. He said to me, "Things are bad, . . . a crisis is looming, . . . indeed already here. When my generation is gone, the extent of this crisis will be exposed."

Sherry Weddell, in *Forming Intentional Disciples*, states something similar: "If this trend does not change, in ten years it will cease to matter that we have a priest shortage."[19] There will be so few Catholics left that the remaining priests will be able to meet their needs.

This can be distressing. We all know people who were raised in Catholic families but have left the practice of the faith. It breaks our hearts. This is especially so with our own children. As the father of six, I know that nothing causes me more pain than my children's struggles with faith and morality. We can be tempted to give in to discouragement and hopelessness.

If you are at all like me, you might find yourself thinking from time to time, *Why me? Why did I have to be born at this time, in this age?* We can feel helpless. How can we fight where there are so many battlefronts? Our efforts to counter the incessant pressures of a thoroughly secular culture can seem futile.

One of my family's favorite reads is J. R. R. Tolkien's *The Lord of the Rings*. The unexpected hero of the story is Frodo Baggins. Frodo finds himself in the midst of a dark world, on a seemingly impossible quest. In one poignant scene, Frodo laments to Gandalf about the times in which they live.

"'I wish it need not have happened in my time,' Frodo. 'So do I,' Gandalf, 'and so do all who live to see such times. But that is not for them to decide. All we have to decide is what to do with the time that is given us.'"[20]

Signs of Hope

What shall we do with the times that are given to us? As followers of Jesus Christ, we are called to be people of faith and hope. Throughout the history of the Church, great outpourings of grace always accompany times of crisis. When things look the bleakest, God acts, and new life springs from the ruins. We live in one of those times.

Cardinal Joseph Ratzinger, before he became Pope Benedict XVI, was a renowned theologian and prefect of the Congregation for the Doctrine of the Faith. He gave a series of interviews on the state of the Church in the post–Vatican II era. The interviews were published in 1985 as *The Ratzinger Report*. At one point, the interviewer asked the cardinal, who was addressing the serious challenges facing the Church, whether he saw any signs of hope. The cardinal said that indeed he did. In particular, he said,

What is hopeful . . . is the rise of new movements which nobody had planned and which nobody has called into being, but which have sprung spontaneously from the inner vitality of the faith itself. What is manifested in them . . . is something like a pentecostal season in the Church. . . . I am now, to an increasing degree, meeting groups of young people in whom there is a wholehearted adhesion to the whole faith of the Church, young people who want to live this faith fully and who bear in themselves a great missionary elan.[21]

New evangelistic movements and initiatives are emerging in our day as signs of great hope, especially among young people. Over the last forty years, we have had the great privilege of leading evangelization initiatives directed toward young people and have witnessed a tremendous reawakening of faith in the lives of countless men and women. Young people are hungry for the gospel. They long to be known and loved unconditionally. They yearn to find meaning and purpose in life. Here are hearts eager and ready for the gospel.

> New evangelistic movements and initiatives are emerging in our day as signs of great hope.

Paul, in his Second Letter to the Corinthians, exhorts us to "look not to the things that are seen but to the things that are unseen; for the things that are seen are transient, but the things that are unseen are eternal" (4:18). The work of the Holy Spirit is not always obvious. It isn't reported on the news.

Our recent popes have prophetically discerned the signs of the times, articulated the crisis, and proposed a renewed vision for the life and mission of the Church precisely in response to this crisis. Pope St. John Paul II is a powerful example of such hope and confidence in the Lord. He prophetically envisioned "a new springtime" of Christian life in the twenty-first century *if* we are docile to the Holy Spirit.[22] The changing landscape of the Church and the culture, however, requires that we seek new ways to reach young people with that good news for which they long.

The challenge can be defined simply: Throughout the Western world, the culture no longer carries the faith, because the culture has become increasingly hostile to the faith. Catholicism can no longer be absorbed by osmosis from the environment, for the environment has become toxic. So we can no longer sit back and assume that decent lives lived in conformity with the prevailing cultural norms will somehow convey the faith to our children and grandchildren and invite others to consider entering the Church.[23]

Pope Francis underlines this point: "I invite everyone to be bold and creative in this task of rethinking the goals, structures, style and methods of evangelization."[24]

Francis is telling us that the status quo is not going to cut it. What was sufficient for passing on the faith and living the faith in our grandparents' generation is inadequate for our day. The approach that says, "We have always done it this way" is insufficient to meet the challenge of proclaiming the gospel today.[25] We need new priorities and methods if we are going to effectively evangelize and form young people as mature, fruitful, and joyful Christian disciples.

Renewal of the Evangelistic Priority

Our Lord's response to the crisis of faith so apparent today is to pour out the gifts and power of the Holy Spirit in abundance and reawaken his Church to her evangelizing call and mission. The Lord is reminding his Church of the Great Commission. Jesus gathered his disciples around him as he prepared to ascend to the Father, and he said,

Go therefore and make disciples of all nations, baptizing them in the name of the Father and of the Son and of the Holy Spirit, teaching them to observe all that I have commanded you; and lo, I am with you always, to the close of the age. (Matthew 28:19-20)

The words of commissioning vary from one Gospel to another, but the message is the same. In Mark's Gospel, Jesus instructs the disciples to "go into all the world and preach the gospel to the whole creation" (16:15). In Matthew they are to "go . . . and make disciples of all nations" (28:19). Luke's account is found in Acts 1, where Jesus instructs his disciples to "wait for the promise of the Father," and then "you shall be my witnesses in Jerusalem and in all Judea and Samaria and to the end of the earth" (1:4, 8).

While there is no explicit account of Jesus' ascension in John's Gospel, we find a similar theme in the farewell discourse at the Last Supper, in John 13–17. Jesus tells his disciples that it is good that he is going away because when he leaves, the Father will send the advocate, the Spirit (see John 16:7). The mission of Jesus will continue through his followers in the power of the Holy Spirit. Later Jesus prays for those who will come to believe in him *through the message of his disciples* (see 17:20). The meaning of his message, in each instance, is simply this: what was accomplished in

> Jesus' life was directed toward bringing the saving mercy and love of the Father to the lost; he commissions us to do the same.

Jesus will be carried to every person, in every generation, by his followers.

Jesus addresses these words *to us today*, not simply to those gathered around him in the Gospel accounts. Jesus' life was directed toward bringing the saving mercy and love of the Father to the lost; he commissions us to do the same. We who follow Jesus Christ are bearers of the message of salvation to the people of our time. And while it is true that Jesus did leave us, he is still with us, "always, to the end of the age" (Matthew 28:20, ESV).

The mission of Jesus continues in us through the power and presence of the Holy Spirit. We are instructed to go; yet before we go, we are to "wait" until we are clothed with power from on high (Acts 1:4). Pope St. John Paul II wrote,

> The Spirit, in fact, makes present in the Church of every time and place the unique Revelation brought by Christ to humanity, making it alive and active in the soul of each individual: "The Counsellor, the Holy Spirit, whom the Father will send in my name, he will teach you all things, and bring to your remembrance all that I have said to you" (Jn 14:26).[26]

Since the Second Vatican Council, the Church has laid out a new approach to and model for evangelization. In 1973, shortly after the council, Pope St. Paul VI penned the encyclical letter *Evangelii Nuntiandi* [Evangelization in the Modern World]. In this letter, he reminds the Church that she "exists in order to evangelize." This is "her deepest identity," her "essential mission."[27]

The call to proclaim the good news of Jesus Christ is once again urgent. This call to evangelize is not new but expresses both the mission of Jesus and his commission to those who follow after him:

The Spirit of the Lord is upon me,
because he has anointed me to preach good news to the poor.
(Luke 4:18)

Pope John Paul II, recognizing the signs of the times, exhorted all the Christian faithful to engage this missionary call: "I sense that the moment has come to commit all of the Church's energies to a new evangelization."[28]

There are people, indeed whole cultures, among whom Christian life was once vibrant but is now diminished because of the relentless winds of secularism. The New Evangelization is a response to this crisis of faith; it recognizes these places as a new mission field where we must proclaim the gospel with renewed fervor and new methods. In this mission field, the evangelization of young people is an urgent priority.

The proposal for a New Evangelization, a defining theme of the pontificates of John Paul II and Benedict XVI, is more than simply a rearranging of our ecclesial furniture; it is a new (renewed) way of thinking and acting.

Archbishop Salvatore Fisichella, president of the Pontifical Council for Promoting the New Evangelization, warns against reducing the New Evangelization to a slogan. It cannot simply be a new heading for what we already do in the Church. It's not simply about rebranding Catholicism. "Tactical changes will not save us."[29] Our task is no less than that of rebuilding and transforming culture, of fostering a civilization of love in the midst of the culture of death. The heart of the New Evangelization is not a new gospel but rather a new mission field.

Historically the Church sent missionaries to evangelize places, cultures, and people who had never heard the gospel. These missionaries proclaimed the good news of Jesus, brought people to conversion, and formed these new believers into Christian communities. Today we are witnessing a new phenomenon. Christian life is eroding in places where historically the Church thrived. This is our new mission field. We need not send missionaries to the far corners of the earth to find an evangelizing mission. The mission field is our own backyard.

The *General Directory for Catechesis* differentiates between the activity of the Church directed toward situations where members "are fervent in their faith and in Christian living" and activity directed toward situations where "entire groups of the baptized have lost a living sense of the faith, or even no longer consider themselves members of the Church, and live a life far removed from Christ and his Gospel."[30] Consequently, Pope Francis calls us to a new mission mindset: "Throughout the world, let us be 'permanently in a state of mission.'"[31]

There and Back Again

I was raised in what was, at that time, a typical Catholic family. Our family life was rich, and though we didn't often explicitly talk about faith, it was evident everywhere. We said our prayers and went to church every Sunday. My parents sacrificed to give us a Catholic education, and when I was old enough, I became an altar server. When asked as a boy what I wanted to be when I grew up, I generally said either a major league baseball player or a priest, and not always in that order.

Looking back, I can see that my Catholic formation was a bit disjointed. My catechesis in grade school was straight out of the *Baltimore Catechism*. My teachers were Franciscan nuns in full habit who lived together in the convent next door to the church. But pop psychology replaced the catechism by the time I started high school, and the religious brothers and sisters who were my educators had shed clerical collars and habits for everyday clothing. In four years of religion class, never once did we read Scripture or a catechism. We did speak about God from time to time, but our teachers rarely mentioned the name of Jesus.

I never encountered the *kerygma*—that simple but powerful proclamation of the gospel that penetrates the heart and calls forth a response. By the age of eighteen, I was indifferent to my Catholic faith, and Sunday Mass was no longer a priority. I was far from God, choosing increasingly to live an immoral life. I could not, however, shed the ultimate questions that kept surfacing in my mind.

The summer after I had graduated from high school, I began spending more time with one of my high school friends, whose parents were experiencing a reawakening of their faith through a new charismatic prayer group at the local parish. I shared some of my struggles and questions about life with this friend. These conversations didn't take place in a church or other faith setting, because neither of us frequented those places.

The change that was taking place in his parents, however, was having some impact on my friend. He suggested that perhaps God was the answer. Through the encouragement of his parents, at the end of that summer, we attended a prayer gathering at an archdiocesan youth center. About two hundred young adults were there, singing and praying in a way that made it seem that they believed God was real and was actually hearing their prayers. Their relationships with one another and their warm welcoming of me were unlike anything I had encountered in my ordinary Church experience. I began a journey over the next months that led to my return to the faith.

Somewhere along this journey, I attended a retreat and heard the gospel proclaimed in a life-changing way. The speaker invited retreatants to respond to the gospel by offering their lives to the Lord and then receiving prayer from the retreat team. I accepted the invitation, some members of the team prayed with me, and I received, in that prayer, the power and presence of the Lord and his love in a way that overwhelmed me. I was filled with a sense of peace and deep joy that seemed to answer my nagging questions. I knew my life would never be the same.

After that, I found myself wanting to pray and read the Scriptures and turn away from my sinful habits. I also experienced a missionary zeal: I wanted to share with others what I had come to know. I returned to the dorms at my college "on mission." The Lord had sent me there to bring his love and mercy to my classmates.

My progress in the Christian life was challenging. In that next year, my dorm mates seemed more successful in drawing me back to my old ways than I was in bringing them to Christ. I realized two things. First, I needed to surround myself with people who would support me in this newfound faith. And second, I needed some formation in order to become a mature disciple.

The Call to Christian Maturity in the New Evangelization

> In our world, often dominated by a secularized culture which encourages and promotes models of life without God, the faith of many is sorely tested, and is frequently stifled and dies. Thus we see an urgent need for powerful proclamation and solid, in-depth Christian formation. There is so much need today for mature Christian personalities, conscious of their baptismal identity, of their vocation and mission in the Church and in the world![32]

When we began our evangelistic initiatives with young people in the 1970s and early 1980s at the St. Paul Catholic Youth

Center, most Catholics were unfamiliar with the term "evangelization" and certainly would not have used it to describe ministry in the Church. Evangelization sounded more Protestant than Catholic. Pope St. John Paul II coined the phrase "new evangelization" in the late 1970s and began using it regularly. Still, it took many years before the terms "evangelize" and the "new evangelization" became known and used commonly in the Church. Today, of course, most serious Catholics and Catholic institutions identify with these terms. More importantly, throughout the Church many evangelistic programs and initiatives have emerged.

Our evangelistic efforts have borne much fruit. One of the greatest joys of our lives has been seeing many thousands of young people come alive in faith and open themselves to the presence and power of the Holy Spirit. Often their faith comes alive through a radical encounter, much like the one I experienced on my retreat. These moments are testimonies to God's manifest presence in the world. When people come to Christ and begin to live their lives in a new way because of that encounter, it strengthens and encourages the faith of others. It's not surprising that there are individuals and ministries dedicated to this initial encounter—to this evangelistic work of witnessing to and proclaiming the gospel and praying with others in their moments of conversion. Our Lord is so eager to have his children come to him that his grace, in these moments, is powerful and abundant.

This experience of the power and love of God has parallels to the experience of Peter, James, and John with Jesus at the transfiguration. "Then Peter said to Jesus, 'Lord, it is good for us to be here; if you wish, I will make three dwellings here, one for you, one for Moses, and one for Elijah'" (Matthew 17:4, NRSVCE).

The transfiguration is a moment of special grace and privileged spiritual experience that "aims at strengthening the apostles' faith in anticipation of [the] Passion" (*Catechism*, 568). It offers a passing glimpse and foreshadowing of the joy of heaven, where Christ will be seen permanently in his eternal glory. The Lord often gives us these special experiences of grace to draw us to himself in conversion and to strengthen our faith. They are not meant to be constant experiences in this life.

We can be tempted, however, to build our faith around the expectation that these experiences will be ongoing. And so too often, when this type of experience goes away, faith can wane. Some who experienced life-changing conversion have, over the years, fallen away from the Lord and the practice of faith. They are like shooting stars that burn brightly for a short time but then fade. As encouraging as it can be to see people come alive in faith, it is equally discouraging to see that faith diminish or disappear altogether.

How can those who seem strong in faith—who begin to reorient their lives around the Lord and his ways and even give themselves generously in mission and service—fall back into sin and abandon the practice of faith? Remaining faithful to the Lord and growing into his likeness over the course of a lifetime is difficult. It requires more than an initial commitment. This is especially so in our current culture, which regularly challenges faith and proposes values contrary to the practice of faith.

Bearing Fruit That Will Last

We are grateful for the tremendous growth of evangelistic initiatives in the Church today. But as urgent as it is to help people enter the Christian life, it is equally important to help them grow in faith. It is also essential to help them find the supportive relationships that they need in order to flourish in the Christian life. If we are to fulfill Jesus' command to "go and bear fruit, fruit that will last" (John 15:16, NRSVCE), the New Evangelization must entail more than a conversion experience. Faith must become *mature*.

The Gospel parable of the sower and the seed illustrates this truth:

> And he taught them many things in parables, and in his teaching he said to them: "Listen! A sower went out to sow. And as he sowed, some seed fell along the path, and the birds came and devoured it. Other seed fell on rocky ground, where it had not much soil, and immediately it sprang up, since it had no depth of soil; and when the sun rose it was scorched, and since it had no root it withered away. Other seed fell among thorns and the thorns grew up and choked it, and it yielded no grain. And other seeds fell into good soil and brought forth grain, growing up and increasing and yielding thirtyfold and sixtyfold and a hundredfold." And he said, "He who has ears to hear, let him hear." (Mark 4:2-9)

In this parable, the seed is the word of God, and the soil is the person who hears that word. Some seed lay on top of the soil, and some fell on hardened ground—neither was able to take root. Similarly, if people fail to receive the word of God—to take it into their lives—it will not take root. Other seed in the parable does take root, but thorns choke the young plant, and it dies. Just so, some people's faith is choked by the cares and temptations of the world and so dies.

Some seed, however, finds fertile soil, sinks deep roots, and produces a plant that grows strong and bears fruit. This is the experience of those who receive help to grow and mature in their newfound faith. If the seeds of faith are to take deep root and bear abundant fruit, we must water, weed, and care for those seeds.

Our mission in the New Evangelization is both to help faith come alive and to assist that faith in becoming mature. Efforts to foster moments of conversion are crucial, but it is just as necessary to assist this newly discovered faith in growing to maturity.

Jesus illustrates this need to grow in foundational aspects of discipleship, insisting in another parable that when we hear the word of God, we must put it into practice. The one who hears the word of God and puts it into practice is like a wise builder who builds his house on a solid foundation, so that when the storms come, the house remains firm. The wise builder is contrasted with the foolish builder, who builds his house on sand and is unprepared when the storms come. His house is washed away (see Matthew 7:24-27). We need to invest in those we evangelize—teaching them, guiding them, bringing them to mature discipleship—so that their lives are built on a firm foundation that will last.

Run so as to Win

In yet a third example, St. Paul compares the Christian life to running a race and competing for a prize. It's obvious, of course, that to compete in a race and finish it requires beginning the race. Those moments of powerful spiritual experience in initial conversion are when the race begins. But we need to do more than just make a good start. Paul warns us that not all who begin the race win the prize. He exhorts us to run so as to win (see 1 Corinthians 9:24).

To win the race, we also need to know where the finish line is and prepare to run so as to reach that goal. We can consider our goals in the work of evangelization in a number of ways. Ultimately, our goal is to help bring those we evangelize into the fullness of God's plan for their lives. The *Catechism of the Catholic Church* expresses this goal for humanity as follows:

> The desire for God is written in the human heart, because man is created by God and for God; and God never ceases to draw man to himself. Only in God will he find the truth and happiness he never stops searching for. (27)

The goal is God himself. This goal is realized finally in the life of eternity in heaven, where we will see God face-to-face, and our communion with him, our becoming "partakers of the divine nature" will be complete (2 Peter 1:4).

What does it mean to "run so as to win" (1 Corinthians 9:24, NABRE)? I (Gordy) enjoy hiking, particularly in the mountains. Years ago, while in Guatemala on a mission trip, some of us decided to hike up to the rim of an inactive volcano that overshadowed the mission site. We could see the top of the volcano from any point in the village, and two of the local people offered to guide us to the peak. We left the next morning at 3:00 a.m.

As the morning wore on, the climbing became increasingly difficult, and some members of our party decided to not continue. I was in good physical condition but wondered whether I could make it to the top. After eight long hours of hiking, we reached the peak, enjoyed the spectacular view, and began our descent. By the time we returned to our camp, it was well into the evening. When I awoke the next morning (and for a few days that followed), I was very sore.

The Christian life is something like hiking up that mountain. We have to be clear about the goal and start the hike. We also need a road map and a guide to show us the way. And we have to be in good spiritual shape if we are going to complete the climb.

The Call to Holiness

Alongside the immediate goal of our evangelistic work, we can speak of a proximate goal. St. Paul describes this goal as to "present everyone mature in Christ":

It is he whom we proclaim, warning everyone and teaching everyone in all wisdom, so that we may present everyone mature in Christ. For this I toil and struggle with all the energy that he powerfully inspires within me. (Colossians 1:28-29, NRSVCE)

Our proximate goal in the New Evangelization is to help those we evangelize to become mature in Christ. The Greek word translated as "mature" in this passage is *teleios*. This term, along with its related noun and verb forms, appears frequently in the New Testament. Jesus uses it in his encounter with the rich young man:

The young man said to him, "All these [commandments] I have observed; what do I still lack?" Jesus said to him, "If you would be perfect [*teleios*], go, sell what you possess and give to the poor, and you will have treasure in heaven; and come, follow me." (Matthew 19:20-21)

The translation of *teleios* as "perfect" can lead to some misunderstanding of the passage. "Perfect," in this context, does not mean without imperfections. No one is perfect, in this sense, in this life. Mature Christian disciples are never completely without sin but are aware of their sinfulness and their need for mercy. Rather, to be perfect, in Jesus' context, is to grow to maturity and begin to act as our heavenly Father acts.

Jesus uses this same word in Matthew 5:48, when he shocks his followers by saying, "You, therefore, must be perfect (*teleios*), as your heavenly Father is perfect." It is on this passage that the Church founds her teaching on the universal call to holiness. This call, a main theme of the Second Vatican Council, is the call for all Christians, *in every state of life*, to be holy. In fact, *Lumen Gentium* [Dogmatic Constitution on the Church], one of the foundational documents from the council, devotes an entire chapter (chapter 5) to this universal call to holiness.

The council fathers were not introducing some new teaching—this call has been constant, beginning with Jesus—but rather reformulating and reproposing this call for Christians today. Over time this call had been obscured by a sense that holiness was reserved for a few. Priests and religious had an obligation to become holy, not the laity.

But what is holiness? Many people think it refers mainly to pious practices such as prayer and other spiritual disciplines. This understanding can lead to a false dichotomy between our spiritual life and the rest of our life. We become holy when we do pious things, such as go to Mass or pray the Rosary. We have our religious box, and holiness goes in that box.

> To be perfect, in Jesus' context, is to grow to maturity and begin to act as our heavenly Father acts.

The holiness to which we are all called, however, has a much broader scope. The *Catechism* identifies holiness with "the fullness of Christian life and . . . the perfection of charity" (2013). The call to holiness is simply the call to live fully the way we were created to live, as creatures made in the image and likeness of God, who is love (see 1 John 4:8). Growing in holiness is growing in love.

The word used for love in this paragraph of the *Catechism* is "charity." Charity, in this sense, encompasses more than sharing what we have with those in need. "Charity is the theological virtue by which we love God above all things for his own sake, and our neighbor as ourselves for the love of God" (*Catechism*, 1822). The holy person is the one who loves perfectly.

Mature disciples love God with their whole heart, soul, mind, and strength, and they love their neighbor as themselves. This is the goal: to become men and women who look like God, the God who is love.

A central theme in the teaching of John Paul II was that this charity to which we are called is a self-giving love. We have the freedom to offer ourselves totally to the Lord in worship and in service to our neighbor, and it is only by exercising that freedom that we enter into and express our created purpose. John Paul II often repeated a phrase from Vatican II, that the human being, "who is the only creature on earth which God willed for itself, cannot fully find himself except through a sincere gift of himself."[33]

In short, this call to holiness, or the perfection of love, involves learning how to grow in our relationship with God in a life of prayer as well as learning what it means to love our neighbor. This encompasses the whole of our lives—how we live each moment; how we speak, eat, use our money, use media, make career choices; and how we conduct ourselves at work. It concerns our sexuality: how we relate as men and women and understand our sexual identity. It concerns how we deal with conflict and resolve wrongdoing. It includes, in fact, the whole of the spiritual, physical, and moral life.

Pope Benedict XVI describes evangelization appropriately in just this sense:

> Human life cannot be realized by itself. Our life is an open question, an incomplete project, still to be brought to fruition and realized. Each man's fundamental question is: How will this be realized—becoming man? How does one learn the art of living? Which is the path toward happiness?
>
> To evangelize means: to show this path—to teach the art of living.[34]

CHAPTER 2

Biblical Patterns of Discipleship

The goal of this chapter is to investigate the biblical patterns of discipleship. We begin by considering the final words that Jesus spoke to his disciples before ascending to heaven—"Go therefore and make disciples of all nations" (Matthew 28:19)—and then explore how Jesus himself provides the pattern for calling and forming disciples.

In this chapter, we go directly to the Gospels to see how Jesus models discipleship, how he himself called and formed disciples, and how he also called his disciples to form and teach other disciples.

Jesus is our primary example of what a disciple should be. Jesus forms his disciples according to the pattern that he displays. It's important to recognize this.

There is in Isaiah a striking prophetic portrait—often called the third "Servant Song"—that shows Jesus to be Someone whose ear is always open to the word of the Lord. He has "an instructed tongue" and speaks only what he hears:

The Lord GOD has given me
   the tongue of those who are taught,
that I may know how to sustain with a word
   him that is weary.
Morning by morning he wakens,
   he wakens my ear
   to hear as those who are taught.
The Lord GOD has opened my ear,
   and I was not rebellious. (Isaiah 50:4-5)

The words that Jesus speaks are not of his own making. He is One who is taught every morning, and he speaks what he hears: "My teaching is not mine, but his who sent me" (John 7:16). And again, "I do nothing on my own authority but speak thus as the Father taught me" (8:28).

The works of Jesus follow this pattern. As a true disciple, Jesus is always looking to his Father in order to carry out his will: "Truly, truly, I say to you, the Son can do nothing of his own accord, but only what he sees the Father doing; for whatever he does, that the Son does likewise" (John 5:19). Jesus is the One "sent" by the Father into the world (7:16). He is the true and perfect disciple who listens, sees, and then does what the Father shows him to do. He constantly has the Father in view, and so he models for us what it means to be his disciples.

> As a true disciple, Jesus is always looking to his Father in order to carry out his will.

As we look to Jesus as our model disciple, let us now try to discern how Jesus called and formed his disciples. We are not looking for a blueprint in the Gospels that lays down precise rules to follow. Nor are we expecting to find a recipe that tells us exactly what ingredients to add together to produce a disciple. We cannot return to the first century and copy what Jesus did in a literal way. Instead, we are seeking to discover *patterns of discipleship* in the biblical text. How did Jesus go about calling his disciples? What strategies did he employ to teach and form them? What can we learn from the record of the Gospels about what Jesus did, so that we are better equipped to call and form disciples in our time?

This chapter, then, is a biblical study focused on what Christ Jesus said and did to form the first batch of disciples. It is foundational for the chapters that follow, each of which will explore how we can call and form disciples in our day after the pattern that Jesus used during his earthly ministry.

The Call to Make Disciples

Jesus didn't just call and form disciples. He also called his disciples to form and teach *other* disciples. His parting words, at the conclusion of Matthew's Gospel, present this commission: "Go therefore and make disciples of all nations, baptizing them in the name of the Father and of the Son and of the Holy Spirit, teaching them to observe all that I have commanded you" (28:19-20).

Who would dare claim the authority to "make disciples" for Jesus and his kingdom, unless Jesus himself had authorized them to do this? If Jesus had not told his chosen followers to do this, it is unlikely that they would have taken the task upon themselves.

The English phrase "make disciples" is only one word in Greek. That word means "to disciple" someone. Matthew is the only Evangelist who uses this word to describe the process of becoming a follower of Jesus. The verse could be translated "Go therefore and *disciple* all the nations."

Matthew uses the same word when describing the scribe of the kingdom of God. He says that "every scribe who has been trained for the kingdom of heaven is like a householder who brings out of his treasure what is new and what is old" (Matthew 13:52). You might ask, Where is the word "make disciples" in this passage? It is translated "has been trained" (other translations say "has been instructed"). The point is that to become a disciple is to be *trained* in the truth and in a way of life. Matthew uses this word a third time to describe Joseph of Arimathea, who "was a disciple of Jesus"—literally, who "was discipled to Jesus" (27:57).

> Discipleship, at its core, is always directed to the person of Jesus. To become a disciple means to enter into a formative relationship with Jesus.

The only other appearance of this verb in the New Testament occurs in Acts 14:21. Paul and Barnabas traveled to the city of Derbe, where they preached the gospel and "made many disciples." By doing this, they directly fulfilled the commission given by Jesus at the end of Matthew's Gospel, to go among the nations and make disciples for Jesus.

At this point, a cautionary question naturally arises: "Do *we* really make disciples for Jesus?" In other words, is this really our work? Can we bring disciples into being?

The short answer is no. Christ Jesus is the One who truly makes disciples. He is the great discipler. That was true when he walked the earth, and it is still true today. Nonetheless, we are called to be coworkers with Jesus as *he* calls and forms disciples. We have a genuine and important part to play in the making of disciples—and this is what we are exploring here.

One important consequence of this is that discipleship must always be directed to the person of Jesus Christ. We don't disciple people to the Church, although the Church is the essential context for discipleship. We certainly don't disciple people to ourselves! Yes, we are called to imitate the saints, and Paul the apostle calls his disciples to imitate him in certain things. But discipleship, at its core, is always directed to the person of Jesus. To become a disciple means to enter into a formative relationship with Jesus.

Let's explore this a bit further. Jesus is preeminently the One who makes disciples, but we have an important part to play. Ours is not a passive role, as if we were sitting by the side of the road and watching while Jesus does the work. We have an active and even creative role in helping others become disciples of Jesus Christ.

The apostle Paul articulates this active role when he says, "I planted, Apollos watered, but God gave the growth" (1 Corinthians 3:6). Paul describes himself as God's coworker (see 3:9). It is God who gives the growth, but we have to plant and water. We have a crucial role in helping others be formed as disciples.

Paul also speaks of himself as "a skilled master builder" who works "according to the commission of God" (1 Corinthians 3:10). He understood himself to be actively shaping and building up the local churches of his day.

This is a crucial truth. We are called to love God and love one another, to live holy lives as we await Christ's return, when he will fully bring his kingdom. But we are also called to be missionaries: to bring the love of God to all people. And this means that we are *also* called to make disciples.

Speaking at the turn of the millennium, Pope St. John Paul II urged all the faithful to embrace the call to make disciples:

> Now, the Christ whom we have contemplated and loved bids us to set out once more on our journey: "Go therefore and make disciples of all nations, baptizing them in the name of the Father, and of the Son and of the Holy Spirit" (Mt 28:19). The missionary mandate accompanies us into the Third Millennium and urges us to share the enthusiasm of the very first Christians.[35]

It's quite revealing that Jesus didn't just say, "Go and announce the gospel to all the nations" (see Mark 16:15). He didn't just say, "Go to all the nations, doing signs and wonders, and manifest the presence of the kingdom" (see 16:17-20). He didn't just say, "Go and show mercy and kindness to all people" (see Matthew 25:34-36).

Certainly we are called to do all these things. But Jesus' final words, as recorded by Matthew, are instructive and important: "Go therefore and *make disciples* of all nations" (28:19, emphasis added). This is more than winning converts or saving souls. It means that we are meant to do for others what Jesus did for his followers: to call them and help form them as disciples of Jesus and coworkers in his mission.

Prerequisite for Discipleship: Conversion to Christ

The phrase "come and see," found in John's Gospel (1:39, 46), captures the starting point for discipleship. You can't become a disciple of Jesus if you don't take the time to come and see what he's all about. When Andrew and another disciple inquired about Jesus, he invited them to "come and see" where he was staying and how he was living: "And they said to him, 'Rabbi' (which means Teacher), 'where are you staying?' He said to them, 'Come and see'" (John 1:38-39).

Andrew then invited his brother Peter, who also came and saw what Jesus was doing. Jesus was a magnetic and powerful person; many people heard about him and came to see what he was all about. These are the crowds who gathered to hear him teach. By coming and seeing what he was doing, they put themselves in a position to be called his disciples.

The same is true today. In one way or another, every potential disciple must come and see what Jesus is all about. They do this by engaging in a conversation or attending a Bible study or having a meal at the house of a Christian friend or attending a church service. Like Zacchaeus, they become disciples by putting themselves in the path of where Christ is passing by (see Luke 19:1-10).

During my last two years in high school, I (Dan) consciously turned down several direct invitations from my good friend Pat to attend his Christian youth group. I wasn't ready to take any steps in my faith, and so I decided *not* to come and see. I missed a real opportunity. Thankfully, God's grace pursued me, and by the time I began college, I was saying yes to similar invitations and finally put myself in the way of encountering Jesus.

> Every potential disciple must come and see what Jesus is all about.

From "encountering" we can move to "conversion." The process of conversion is like a bridge that takes us from life apart from Christ to the life of a disciple. Sometimes conversion seems to happen all at once, but normally there is a process that leads someone to faith in Jesus and commitment to follow him.[36] Today we commonly describe this process in terms of an encounter with the Person of Jesus and with the power of the Holy Spirit.

According to Pope Benedict XVI,

> Being Christian is not the result of an ethical choice or a lofty idea, but the encounter with an event, a person, which gives life a new horizon and a decisive direction.[37]

As we draw near, Christ meets us and calls us through an encounter with himself. By receiving his invitation and responding to this encounter with faith, we cross the bridge and walk onto the path of discipleship. In stories throughout the Gospels, we see examples of Jesus encountering people and calling them to follow him. He is doing the very same thing today.

Acknowledging, then, the central place of conversion, let's return to our main topic: what do we learn from Jesus' example about what it means to follow him as a disciple?

Biblical Patterns of Discipleship

In order to investigate biblical patterns of discipleship, we will seek to answer the following questions: What is a disciple? What does it take to become a disciple of Jesus? What are the primary qualities or marks of a disciple that we find in the pages of the Gospels? What are the approaches or strategies that Jesus used in forming his own disciples? What can we learn from these for the task of calling and forming disciples today?

We can identify seven patterns that display what disciples are and how Jesus called and formed them. There are undoubtedly other illuminating ways to organize the patterns for discipleship found in the pages of the Gospels, but these are the ones on which we will focus:

1. A disciple is one who decides to follow after Jesus.
2. A disciple is one who is taught and tutored by Jesus.
3. Discipleship includes hands-on training and testing.
4. Disciples are formed in the context of a community of disciples.

5. Training in discipleship includes being sent out on mission.
6. Jesus worked with groups of different sizes in forming his disciples.
7. Jesus led his disciples through an intensive period of formation to equip them for lifelong discipleship and fruitfulness.

Following a discussion of these seven patterns, we will conclude the chapter by pointing to the goal of this activity: What was Jesus hoping to produce by forming disciples and pouring out his Spirit on them?

1. A disciple is one who decides to follow after Jesus.

It is striking how frequently the language of "following" appears in the context of discipleship in all four Gospels. The first disciples—Andrew, Peter, James, John, and Matthew—all heard the same call from Jesus: "Follow me" (Matthew 4:19-20; 9:9). As Edward Sri points out,

> Discipleship was . . . an apprenticeship—an immersion into the rabbi's whole way of life. . . .
> Disciples were expected to follow their rabbi so closely that they would be covered with their master's whole way of thinking, living, and acting.[38]

So becoming a Christian disciple is more than just being a religious person or holding a set of religious beliefs. If we are disciples, we actually follow a person—and that Person is Jesus Christ.

When the rich young man approached Jesus, he asked how he should live, and Jesus told him, "Keep the commandments." On hearing this, the young man brightened up because he had been following the commandments since his youth. All seemed well until Jesus added these words: "If you would be perfect, go, sell what you possess and give to the poor, and you will have treasure in heaven; and come, follow me" (Matthew 19:21). The young man, we are told, went away sad because he was not able to respond to this discipleship call.

An essential trait of discipleship is full identification with Jesus. Any of us can choose high religious and moral ideals—and these are good. But we can decide for these on our own and set our own standards; we don't have to follow Jesus or anyone else. To be a Christian disciple, however, means to set out to follow Jesus. It means sharing his fate and identifying fully with him.

It is always Jesus who calls us to follow him and be his disciples: "You did not choose me, but I chose you" (John 15:16). To be apprenticed as Jesus' disciples isn't something that we volunteer for from our high and noble motives. The initiative isn't with us, even if at times it seems to be.

On one occasion, a man presented *himself* to Jesus and said that he would follow him (see Matthew 8:19-20; Luke 9:57-58). Jesus immediately put him to the test, to see whether he was really ready to follow in his steps unconditionally and be counted among his company. The source of discipleship, then, is Christ's grace-filled call.

For our part, we are invited to make a generous response. But the origin of discipleship is always Jesus' call, and the engine of discipleship is his grace. This is essential: if we are called, then we should have confidence that with the call will come the grace to fulfill it. If the initiative lies with us—if discipleship is a burden that we take on our backs—then we are left to rely on our own resources—our strength, goodness, faithfulness, power. And we know how fleeting and fragile these are. Only if the call comes from Jesus can we be assured that we will receive (as a gift) the grace and help to fulfill this call.

To sum up, in Jesus' day, to follow him had real consequences. It was costly and required commitment. To become a disciple of Jesus meant leaving home and family and setting out on the road, walking behind Jesus and identifying with his company of friends. Today we don't follow Jesus physically, by strapping on our sandals and walking behind him down the dusty roads of Palestine, but we are genuinely called to follow him.

For me (Dan), the call to follow Jesus as his disciple came when I left my home and began my first year at the university. I had my life pretty well mapped out, with clear career paths in mind. Of course, I wanted to pursue these plans as a good person who believed in God and basically lived a good life, but I still had a firm grip on my plans for my life. But then this person, Jesus, whom I had effectively quarantined at a safe distance, burst into my life and became real and living. I began to experience his word and his presence; prayer came alive and became a two-way street. I realized that I was dealing with a living and active God who knew me by name and possibly had a plan for my life that might not line up with my own.

I genuinely wrestled: *Was I willing to cast in my lot and follow Jesus, staking my whole life on him and his promises?* I was not as quick as James and John to lay down my nets. My response was halting, with stops and starts and reconsiderations.

Without the example and encouragement of other disciples, I doubt that I would have given my life over to Christ fully and decided to follow him. I realize in hindsight (with a shudder) how easily I could have opted out and gone my own way. Eventually, through the prayers of many, I was able to experience the joy of the man who discovered buried treasure and sold all he had to obtain that treasure (see Matthew 13:44).

So the first mark of a Christian disciple is that he or she—eventually and intentionally—"follows after" Jesus.

2. A disciple is one who is taught and tutored by Jesus.

There's a good reason why the disciples of Jesus often address him as "Rabbi," or "Teacher." John the Evangelist tells us that the title "Rabbi" means "Teacher" (1:38). Literally, *rabbi* is "my master": it was a common term used by disciples in Jesus' time to address their master, or teacher.

Even more frequently, Jesus' disciples and many others address him simply as "Teacher." It's a title that Jesus adopts:

"You call me Teacher and Lord; and you are right, for so I am" (John 13:13).

The Gospels make it clear that Jesus spent a lot of time teaching. He often taught large crowds of people, once climbing into a boat so that he could address all the people gathered on the shore (see Mathew 13:2). In the lead-up to the Sermon on the Mount, Jesus was surrounded by crowds of people. He climbed the mountain and then "sat down" (5:1), taking up the conventional posture of a teacher. His disciples came to him to be instructed: "And he opened his mouth and taught them" (5:2).

At first blush, it appears that only Jesus' chosen disciples were privy to this astonishing teaching, but at the end of the Sermon on the Mount, we learn that the crowds were also listening in on what he was saying: "And when Jesus finished these sayings, the crowds were astonished at his teaching, for he taught them as one who had authority" (Matthew 7:28-29).

Jesus also took his disciples aside on many occasions and explained to them his teaching in parables. He opened his mind to them and revealed things about the kingdom of God. This teaching was progressive, one thing building on another. The disciples were often slow learners, failing to understand Jesus' purpose. But he persevered in patience, instructing them so that they would be ready to carry on his mission.

Jesus' goal is neatly captured in a verse from Luke's Gospel: "A disciple is not above his teacher, but every one when he is fully taught will be like his teacher" (6:40). Jesus' goal is that the disciples be "fully taught" by taking on his mind and heart.

This teaching occurred on two levels. At times Jesus gave "systematic" teaching about an area. Examples of this are found in the Sermon on the Mount (see Matthew 5–7) and in the missionary discourse of Matthew 10. But more often, Jesus gave instructions in the midst of concrete events, taking advantage of circumstances to instruct his disciples.

So when James and John privately expressed their wish to be his top men, Jesus corrected them and took advantage of the opportunity to instruct all his disciples about taking the lowest place (see Mark 10:35-45). When the disciples pushed the children away in order to protect their master, he corrected them, teaching that the kingdom of God is suited exactly to those who approach with a childlike humility of heart (see Matthew 19:13-15).

Today we can continue to be taught by Jesus if we open our ears and come to him day by day. He continues to speak in the Scriptures, through the Church, and through the Holy Spirit in our hearts. Jesus promises that the Holy Spirit will continue to teach his disciples: "But the Counselor, the Holy Spirit, whom the Father will send in my name, he will teach you all things, and bring to your remembrance all that I have said to you" (John 14:26).

The Son and the Spirit remain the *primary* teachers for Christian disciples. But the disciples also teach others; teaching is part of forming disciples. In his final commission, Jesus instructs the Twelve to teach the new disciples all that he has commanded them to observe (see Matthew 28:20). As the very first Christian community takes shape after Pentecost, we are told, these first Christians "devoted themselves to the apostles' teaching and fellowship, to the breaking of bread and the prayers" (Acts 2:42).

As we shall see, teaching plays an important part in the formation of Christian disciples, Teaching is not everything—it is not the whole of disciple making—but it provides a central plank in the foundation. It has both a doctrinal aspect and a practical way-of-life aspect. Jesus continually taught his disciples about the Father, about himself and the work of salvation, and about the "other Counselor" who comes to us (the Holy Spirit). But he also instructed them about how they were to live, how they needed to forgive one another, and how they were to take the lowest place in service.

We too need to be taught by Jesus and the Spirit—and by our fellow disciples—if we are to reach maturity and be ready for mission.

3. Discipleship includes hands-on training and testing.

If teaching provides one essential element in Jesus' approach to disciple making, then hands-on training and testing supply another. Yes, Jesus was typically the main event wherever he went: he did most of the teaching and performed the majority of the signs and wonders among the people. This makes sense: he is the Word made flesh announcing and ushering in the kingdom of God. But his disciples were not just passive bystanders. Jesus often included them in his ministry and used situations that arose as training opportunities.

One evening, after a full day of ministering to crowds of people, Jesus decides to cross over to the other side of the Sea of Galilee. While he and his disciples are in the boat, a fierce storm blows in, and the boat, filling with water, begins to founder. Jesus, meanwhile, is asleep on a cushion! Terrified that they will sink, the disciples wake him with words of complaint: "Teacher, do you not care if we perish?" (Mark 4:38).

Jesus arises, calms the storm and the waves with a word, and then admonishes the disciples for their lack of faith: "Why are you afraid? Have you no faith?" (Mark 4:40). As this case study shows, Jesus allows events to challenge his disciples so that he can train them in the kind of faith they will need in order to weather the storms that will come upon them.

The feeding of the five thousand also provides a marvelous example of hands-on training. Jesus, the disciples, and a very large crowd of people are situated in a deserted area, far from available food supplies. Judging that a crisis is looming, the disciples approach Jesus and ask him to send the crowds away, to the surrounding villages, so that they will be able to find food. Instead of following their counsel, Jesus turns the tables and challenges the disciples: "They need not go away; you give them something to eat" (Matthew 14:16).

Jesus knows very well that the disciples cannot supply food for so many. He is testing and training them.

The disciples hunt around and come up with five loaves of bread and two fish—a ridiculously inadequate supply of food for five thousand and more people. But then Jesus speaks the crucial words: "Bring them here to me" (Matthew 14:18). He then blesses the meager rations and instructs *his disciples* to distribute the food. After the entire crowd is fully fed, it turns out that there is more food left over than what they had at the start.

This is more than a provision of food; Jesus *involves* his disciples in this miracle, teaching them that they have a crucial role to play in "feeding" the people. Only Jesus can multiply the bread—and only he can provide the true "bread from heaven" (John 6:32)—but the disciples learn that they are to be coworkers with Jesus. Is this not a lesson in which every disciple needs to be trained? What Jesus did then for his disciples, he continues to do for us today.

The examples of hands-on training are numerous. We find Peter stepping out of the boat to come to Jesus but sinking when his eyes fix on the waves (see Matthew 14:28-32). Martha is instructed about the "good portion" when she complains to Jesus that her sister is not doing her share of the work (see Luke 10:38-42). The disciples are taught about the realities of spiritual warfare when they fail to cast out a demon from a possessed man and wonder why their efforts didn't work (see Mark 9:14-29).

On one occasion, toward the conclusion of his public ministry, Jesus actively tests the disciples' faith and knowledge in order to draw from them the kind of faith and trust that he seeks. He gathers them and asks, "What are people saying about me? Who do they say I am?" They list the various opinions that people are expressing. Then he puts the question directly to them: "Who do you say that I am?" (Matthew 16:15).

Simon Peter steps forward and gives an answer (the true answer!) that reveals God's work in him: "You are the Christ, the Son of the Living God" (Matthew 16:16). Based on this, Jesus then tells Peter that he will play a critical role: he will be the rock upon which Jesus will build his Church.

But then, when Jesus says that he is to suffer and die in Jerusalem, Peter takes Jesus aside and begins to rebuke him. Clearly he feels a new confidence in himself, such that he can begin to instruct the Master. In response, Jesus rebukes Peter and chastises his unenlightened zeal. In one brief training episode, Jesus both establishes Peter in his future role and sharply corrects him, all the while revealing to the other disciples who he really is and what he must suffer.

To repeat: we cannot duplicate this hands-on training by following Jesus around the roads of first-century Palestine, but if we let him, Jesus will train us as disciples through the various circumstances of our lives. He tests and trains us directly but also through the agency of other disciples so that we will be ready to work alongside him, in company with our fellow disciples, in the work of the kingdom.

As a nineteen-year-old just setting out on the path of discipleship, I (Dan) received my own hands-on training in what it means to step out in faith. One winter evening, I was roused from my dorm room by two desperate young women who were unable to open the doors of their car. (A cold rain had frozen the doors shut.) I soon found myself outside in a driving snow, helplessly tugging at the doors as my hands became increasingly numb.

Realizing that the attempt to open the doors was probably futile, I suggested that the two women go inside to get warm while I tried one last time to unseal the doors. But the doors would not budge, and I pretty much gave up. Just then a quiet voice spoke in my mind: "Why don't you ask for God's help to open the doors?" My immediate internal response was that God had better things to do than open frozen car doors, and so I dismissed the idea. But being rather desperate, I soon decided to give prayer a try.

I went to the passenger-side door, prayed that God would open it on the count of three, grabbed the handle, counted to three, and gave a tug—and the door flew open. I was astonished. But being skeptical (like Gideon—see Judges 6:36), I then asked for the same result with the *other* frozen door. I walked around the car, prayed, counted to three, gave a tug on the door handle—and this door too flew open.

I stood amazed and then went back inside, able to give the two women the good news and tell them about how the car doors opened as an answer to prayer. For me, as for the disciples in the sinking boat, this was an invaluable hands-on lesson about the power of God to act, even in small things. It's a lesson I have never forgotten.

4. Disciples are formed in the context of a community of disciples.

When we read the Gospels, we often miss something obvious: Jesus forms his disciples not one-on-one in a solitary way but in the context of a community of disciples. Because we are (rightly) so entranced by the words and actions of Jesus, we often lose sight of the fact that he almost always speaks and acts in the company of his disciples—sometimes with three of them, sometimes with twelve, sometimes with seventy or more.

Consider some examples. When Jesus reveals to Nathaniel his messianic identity, he does so in the company of Philip and probably others (see John 1:47-51). It is to the *twelve* apostles, huddled together in a boat, that Jesus appears walking on the water, teaching them what it means to put their faith into action (see Matthew 14:22-27). When James and John secretly approach Jesus to request the first and second places in his kingdom, the other ten hear about this request and are understandably miffed at James and John; Jesus then brings them *all* together and teaches them what service in the kingdom must be like (see Mark 10:35-45). Time and again, Jesus speaks to the group of disciples, instructing them through parables and teaching them about the kingdom of God.

We might (wrongly) conclude that Jesus was merely using an effective pedagogical approach for individual training, because he knew that people learn best in groups and through the experiences, and even failures, of others. But this is not all that is going on. Jesus is not just forming individual disciples in the context of a communal environment; he is genuinely forming a community of disciples by forming them together. The goal isn't just the personal formation of each disciple. The communal context is not just a means to an end. A crucial part of the goal is the communal formation of all together.

Jesus is forming a new family, the people of God. The various goals that Jesus may have—personal formation, communal formation, training in mission, growth in character—are all fulfilled in a communal context because forming the Church into the body of Christ and the people of God is the goal.

In a letter to seminarians, Pope Benedict draws attention to the importance of this communal context for discipleship: "One does not become a priest on one's own. The 'community of disciples' is essential, the fellowship of those who desire to serve the greater Church."[39]

This communal context is displayed in Jesus' words and actions on the night before his death. What is the first thing Jesus does when they are gathered together for a final meal? He takes off his outer garments and—inexplicably—washes the feet of each of his disciples. Masters do not wash the feet of their disciples; this was a role reserved for slaves. But Jesus does this as an example to them all because this is how they must act toward one another as a company of disciples (see John 13:1-20).

Next, Jesus gives the disciples a commandment: to love one another. By this others will know that they are his disciples (see John 13:34-35). We can only love one another in a communal context; we cannot do this on our own. The primary proof that *Christ* is among us—the love that we show to one another—requires that we be together as a company of disciples.

We are tempted to read the final discourse in John's Gospel in an individual way, but what Jesus says, he says to *all* those gathered, and his words only make sense in a communal setting. The words he speaks apply to each of the disciples *personally*, but they are to be fulfilled among the disciples corporately. His words and prayers make no sense apart from this communal context. Together we are his friends, and together we are called to lay down our lives for each other (see John 15:12-17).

In Jesus' final prayer, he prays for all the disciples as a group, that they may be one and united (see John 17:11), that they may be kept from the evil one (see 17:15), and that they may be sanctified in the truth (see 17:17). It is by virtue of the unity of the disciples that Christ and the Father are most powerfully revealed to the world (see 17:22-24).

This does not mean that God cannot form us and train us through our own personal experiences and circumstances. Of course he can, and he does. But we are tempted to think about discipleship as a personal project that we do on our own, that happens just between us and God. This is not the biblical pattern that we see in the life of Jesus.

Jesus typically teaches and forms his disciples in a communal setting, as a people who by their love for one another reveal Jesus to the world. Recapturing this communal context for discipleship is an important step in the task of forming Christian disciples today.

5. Training in discipleship includes being sent out on mission.

There is a perennial temptation to think that Christians should be sent out on mission only after they have been fully trained as disciples: first comes the formation in discipleship, and then we are sent out on mission. But this is not the pattern we see in the Gospels.

True enough, Jesus does not seem to send his disciples out on mission on their first or second day; he keeps them with him for a period of initial formation. But even in these early days, the disciples accompany Jesus as he engages in mission, and he involves them in simple ways. The first stage of missionary training is accompanying Jesus as he proclaims the kingdom of God. Today this involves accompanying other trained disciples as they engage in mission.

Then at a certain point, when Jesus sees that the disciples are ready, he sends them out two by two, away from him and on their own. They were probably filled with competing emotions of hopeful anticipation and terror. In Matthew 10 (called the "missionary discourse"), Jesus calls the Twelve together and imparts to them his own spiritual authority to heal and to cast out unclean spirits. Then he instructs them about their mission—what they should expect, how they should act in certain circumstances—and sends them out.

How did things turn out for the disciples? Luke tells us that they went through many villages, preaching the good news of the kingdom and healing people in every place (see 9:6). Mark records that they preached repentance to the people, cast out many demons, and healed many people through anointing with oil (6:12-13).

Luke records a further sending out of seventy disciples to announce the coming of the kingdom of God. Upon their return, they are filled with joy because, in the name of Jesus, even the demons are subject to them. Jesus too rejoices in prayer to the Father when he sees the works of the kingdom done by his disciples. But he tells the seventy to rejoice not because demons are subject to them but because the disciples belong to God (see Luke 10:17-20).

The disciples did not always experience success—and this too is important for training in mission. When Jesus returned with Peter, James, and John from the Mount of Transfiguration, he found his disciples involved in a dispute because they were unable to cast out a demon. After Jesus cast out the spirit and healed the afflicted child, his disciples approached him privately and asked why they were unable to cast out the unclean spirit. Jesus pointed to their lack of faith (see Matthew 17:20), but he also spoke of the spiritual effort—both prayer and fasting—needed in certain cases (Mark 9:29). We often learn more from our failures in mission than from our successes.

Pope Francis, underlining the need to be engaged in mission even before training in discipleship is completed, points to the patterns found in the New Testament:

> [L]et us look at those first disciples, who, immediately after encountering the gaze of Jesus, went forth to proclaim him joyfully: "We have found the Messiah!" (Jn 1:41). The Samaritan woman became a missionary immediately after speaking with Jesus, and many Samaritans come to believe in him "because of the woman's testimony" (Jn 4:39). So too, Saint Paul, after his encounter with Jesus Christ, "immediately proclaimed Jesus" (Acts 9:20).[40]

My (Dan's) experience matches this biblical pattern. The whole idea of mission—of speaking to other people about Jesus or about my faith—terrified me. Then two things happened. First, I experienced the presence and power of the Holy Spirit in my life, and suddenly my mouth was opened, like the disciples' on the day of Pentecost (see Acts 2). But second, I began accompanying other disciples, watching them as they welcomed people, spoke to them, and gave public testimony to what God had done in their lives. Then it was my turn. At the start, I was mostly terrified, but I began inviting my friends and acquaintances to Christian events, and I spoke to them about what God had done in my life.

I vividly recall the first time I was "sent out" on mission. I was asked (with another student) to publicize and lead a Bible study in a dormitory well-known for its secular mind-set. We posted flyers, prepared the Bible study, made our way to the room we had reserved—*and no one showed up.* I was both disappointed and mildly relieved! But within two years, I was leading an active Bible study with student leaders in my dorm and engaging in one-on-one Bible studies on the Old Testament with a Jewish friend. Through both failure and (some) success, I learned something about what it means to be sent out on mission, needing to rely on Christ and the power of the Spirit every step of the way.

6. Jesus worked with groups of different sizes in forming his disciples.

The question of "structures" confronts us as we seek to form disciples today. How should disciple making be structured? What kinds of groups do we need, and what is the most effective way to multiply the number of disciples for the work of mission?

We can't expect to receive precise answers to these questions from the pages of the Bible; Jesus does not give us a strict program to follow. But we can discern patterns in how Jesus worked with people in different-sized groupings, and from this we can gain important insight into forming disciples today.

Let's begin with the largest circle: Jesus attracted large crowds of people wherever he went. Whether in villages or in the countryside, hundreds and even thousands of people came out to hear him and to see the works that he was doing. He was a big attraction. This, of course, got the attention of the leadership class: they too came to hear him and interrogate him because he was having such an impact on the people.

Jesus seems to have welcomed the crowds: he didn't flee from them or send them away. Instead, he spoke to them, proclaimed the good news of the kingdom, healed them, and delivered them from spiritual powers that bound them. This was an important part of his ministry; it gave profound witness to who he was and what he had come to do.

When Jesus stood up to read in the synagogue in Nazareth (his hometown), he chose the text from Isaiah 61:1-2 and announced that this was now being fulfilled in him:

"The Spirit of the Lord is upon me,
because he has anointed me to preach good news to the poor.
He has sent me to proclaim release to the captives
and recovering of sight to the blind,
to set at liberty those who are oppressed,
to proclaim the acceptable year of the Lord." (Luke 4:18-19)

But it is important to recognize that preaching to large crowds was not Jesus' primary strategy for building up the Church or preparing for a worldwide spread of the Gospel. The people in the crowds did not become disciples by virtue of being in the crowd, though it was often *from* these crowds that future disciples were drawn. The Gospels show, in fact, that Jesus recognized the unreliability of the crowds and their responses (see John 2:23-25; 6:26). In terms of disciple making, large groups have a role to play, but it is most often a preparatory role.

As many scholars and pastors have recognized, Jesus' primary strategy was to call and work intensely with a small group of people and, through them, to impact the wider world.[41] Crucially, Jesus selected his disciples only after spending the entire night in prayer (see Luke 6:12). Pope Benedict notes this:

We should pay close attention to the way that Jesus called his closest associates to proclaim the Kingdom of God (cf. *Lk* 10:9). In the first place, it is clear that the first thing he did was to pray for them: before calling them, Jesus spent the night alone in prayer, listening to the will of the Father.[42]

The primary grouping Jesus worked with was the twelve apostles; these became the main public witnesses to his ministry. They stayed with him, traveled with him, shared his food, and lived from a common purse (see John 13:29). The Twelve were the constant recipients of Jesus' teaching and hands-on training. After the death of Judas Iscariot, the apostles chose another close disciple of Jesus, Matthias, to fill the missing slot (see Acts 1:15-26).

A close reading of the Gospels shows that there were both larger and smaller circles along with the Twelve. We hear of the seventy disciples that Jesus gathered and sent out on mission toward the end of his ministry, as he was approaching Jerusalem. Matthias was probably chosen from this wider network of disciples. We also hear of many women who accompanied Jesus, who would have heard much of his teaching and who became the very first "apostles" of the resurrection.

> If we are to work with Jesus in making disciples, we have to adopt his strategy of working closely with a few for the sake of the many.

From the Twelve, Jesus on occasion took aside three—Peter, James, and John—for special companionship and training. They alone were invited to join Jesus when he raised the ruler's daughter from the dead (see Mark 5:37; see Luke 8:51); they alone accompanied Jesus up the mountain and experienced his transfiguration (see Matthew 17:1); they alone were invited to stay near Jesus during his agonizing prayer in the Garden of Gethsemane (see Mark 14:33)—and they failed to stay awake!

And even among these three, Jesus worked especially with Peter: testing him (see Matthew 14:28-31), correcting him (16:22-23), assigning him a special role in the Church (16:17-19), and personally reestablishing him after his three-fold denial (John 21:15-19).

What are we to conclude from Jesus' pattern of working with different groups of disciples (one, three, twelve, and seventy)? In certain cases, the number chosen has a symbolic significance, not just a practical usefulness. The twelve apostles clearly reflect the twelve tribes of Israel: by establishing twelve primary apostles, Jesus shows that his mission is to reconstitute the people of Israel around himself. The number seventy probably reflects the number of Israelites who went down to Egypt (see Genesis 46:27; see Exodus 1:5) but also the number of elders who attended Moses on the mountain and who received a portion of the Spirit of God for the pastoral care of the people (see Exodus 24:1; see Numbers 11:16-25).

But the point is not to form groups of exactly the same size as Jesus did, as if there were something magical about these numbers. We draw two insights from seeing how Jesus worked with different-sized groupings.

First, Jesus used several different structures concurrently to form and train his disciples, sometimes working with a relatively larger group (seventy), sometimes working with very few (three). Crucially, these groups were small enough that Jesus could have a close personal relationship with each of the members, and they could gather around him for teaching and hands-on training.

Second, Jesus did his primary disciple making in these small groups, not with the large crowds. This is an obvious point but well worth emphasizing. There is always a pull to reach the multitudes and to draw in large crowds. When thousands of people attend an event, it's encouraging—and should be. But the lesson from the Gospels is that disciples cannot be formed *except* through this attention to small groups, where individual disciples can receive personal training. If we are to work with Jesus in making disciples, we have to adopt his strategy of working closely with a few for the sake of the many.

7. Jesus led his disciples through an intensive period of formation to equip them for life-long discipleship and fruitfulness.

The process of spiritual growth as a disciple of Christ never ends. We are always able, by God's grace, to advance in holiness and be transformed into the image of God. For this we need what Dietrich von Hildebrand called "the readiness to change." This unreserved readiness to change not only characterizes the beginning of our path in discipleship. "It also constitutes the permanent basis for continual progress on our road."[43] This was true for the first disciples of Christ and remains true for us today.

Yet the Gospels also demonstrate the importance of a specific period of formation, of apprenticeship. They show us that Jesus worked intensely with his chosen disciples, preparing them for their ongoing mission in the world. We don't know exactly how long Jesus worked with the Twelve (and the seventy), but the Gospel of John indicates a period of about three years, marked by three Passover feasts. This is a substantial period of time but still limited.

Often people describe the path of discipleship in two stages: the first stage is responding to Jesus' call, leaving our nets behind, and following him; the second stage is the rest of our lives, as we follow Jesus across a span of years. This two-stage process does in fact describe something important about how discipleship works, but it omits the essential period of formation through which Jesus led his disciples.

As Jesus approached the final days of his earthly life, he gathered his close disciples—the Twelve—for a special meal. The Last Supper provided a final occasion for Jesus to hand on crucial aspects of his work, preparing his apostles for when he would no longer walk among them. He washed their feet, teaching them how to serve one another (see John 13:1-20; Luke 22:24-27), and he established the Eucharist as the ongoing participation in his Body and Blood, to be done in remembrance of him. He also addressed them as his faithful disciples who had remained with him throughout his ministry: "You are those who have continued with me in my trials" (Luke 22:28).

The Gospel of John records the long dialogue at the Last Supper between Jesus and the Twelve, as Jesus wraps up this intense period of personal formation (see 13–17). He is about to leave them, but he imparts his peace to them and promises the gift of the Holy Spirit (see 14:25-27). He reminds them that they must be joined to him as branches to the vine and demonstrates what it means for them to love him and one another (see 15:1-17). Jesus prepares his disciples to carry on without his physical presence, commending them to the Father and promising that he will guard them, keep them faithful, and make them fruitful (see 17:1-26).

Jesus offers in the Gospels a *pattern* for how disciples are formed. The example of the apostle Paul offers insight into this process of apprenticeship as it unfolded in the early Church. Paul typically took disciples with him on his mission trips—living with them, working alongside them, and forming them as missionary disciples to carry on the work. Paul's letters to Timothy and Titus reveal Paul in his role as a spiritual father, shaping the lives and ministries of these two younger associates. The letters provide a treasure trove of wisdom for how to go about forming missionary disciples. And in his Letter to the Philippians, Paul calls the Philippians to imitate him and to follow his example (see 3:17). This is the language of discipleship.

There are many examples of this sort of approach in the history of the Church. The great paradigm appears in the early monastic movement (fourth and fifth centuries), when apprentices sought out seasoned monks for instruction on how to live an ascetic life in the desert. The great monastic rules and an ongoing pattern of formation in a way of life arose from these informal arrangements.

Today we have specific periods of formation for priests, deacons, and those in religious communities. Many new movements in the Church—the Neocatechumenal Way, Focolare,

Emmanuel Community, Communion and Liberation, to name a few—have a specific period of formation for people considering their missionary community way of life. When we think of training for ministry in the Church or preparation for religious or lay communities, this period of focused formation seems to make the most sense.

But does it have any place in the forming of lay missionary disciples in the broader Church? We believe that it does. Deliberate formation greatly enriches the quality and depth of discipleship, equipping those who receive such training for a lifelong pursuit of holiness as disciples.

The Goal: A Community of Mature Missionary Disciples

If our call is to work with Christ in the power of the Spirit to form Christian disciples, then how do we express our goal? We could say that our goal is to form Christian disciples who consistently fulfill the command to love God and neighbor. We could say that our goal is to help form Christian disciples who show the fruits of faith, hope, and love. Or perhaps our goal is to form Christian disciples who seek to grow in holiness and to be transformed into the image of Christ. All of these are central goals of the Christian life, and they capture an important part of our task.

But we would like to offer another way of stating the goal of Christian discipleship, a way that captures important elements of the biblical vision for discipleship and contributes to our efforts to bring about a new evangelization. The goal is to form *a community of mature missionary disciples of Christ.*

Pope Francis describes the evangelizing Church as "a community of missionary disciples who take the first step, who are involved and supportive, who bear fruit and rejoice."[44] Francis identifies the need "for ongoing formation and maturation" if this call to worldwide mission is to be successful.[45]

Using similar language, George Weigel speaks of the need for "a mission-centered community of disciples with a clear sense of identity and purpose" if we are to reach the postmodern world.[46] We have shown how important community and mission are for discipleship. To conclude this chapter, we would like to attend to Francis' call for maturation by summing up what the New Testament has to say about maturity in Christian discipleship.

At first glance, it would seem that the Bible has very little to say about maturity as such—the term appears only two or three times in the most common English translations of the New Testament. But despite this infrequency, the term "maturity" very effectively captures the goal of discipleship in the New Testament.

On several occasions, for instance, Scripture tells us to leave behind childish ways and advance to spiritual maturity. Paul tells the Corinthians that they are still "babes in Christ" rather than the spiritual disciples they ought to be (1 Corinthians 3:1). Because of this, he needs to feed them milk instead of solid food (see 3:2).

Later in the same letter, Paul encourages his readers: "Do not be children in your thinking; be babes in evil, but in thinking be mature" (1 Corinthians 14:20). The Letter to the Hebrews uses the same metaphor, telling readers that by this time they ought to be teachers, but they remain unskilled in the truth and so need to be fed with milk, like babes (see 5:12-13). The author calls them to leave behind the elementary foundation and move on to "maturity" (see 6:1).

Likewise, when Jesus speaks about the seed sown among thorns, he says that "their fruit does not mature" (Luke 8:14). The seed springs up but fails to ripen and bear fruit.

Consider how the apostle Paul describes the goal of his apostolic ministry: "Him we proclaim, warning everyone and teaching everyone with all wisdom, that we may present everyone mature in Christ" (Colossians 1:28, ESV). This is striking: Paul's goal *in this life* is to help bring each disciple of Christ to maturity. The key word Paul uses here is the Greek term, *teleios* (perfect), which we have considered previously.

Essentially then, we start out as infants in our faith but are meant to grow to adulthood. Paul uses this metaphor of growth from infancy to adulthood when explaining that the spiritual gifts are given to build up the body of Christ, "until all of us come to the unity of the faith and of the knowledge of the Son of God, to maturity, to the measure of the full stature of Christ. We must no longer be children" (Ephesians 4:13-14, NRSVCE). When appealing to the Philippians, he speaks in a way that assumes they have reached the spiritual maturity capable of responding to his words: "Let those of us then who are mature be of the same mind" (Philippians 3:15, NRSVCE).

When we say that the goal of Christian discipleship is maturity, we are describing Christian men and women who have been formed and tested as disciples and are ready to be sent out on mission. Crucially, they are now able to help form other disciples: they can only give what they have received.

All of us, even when we become mature disciples, continue to grow and need to grow. As Tom Bergler writes in *From Here to Maturity*: "Far from being the end point of spiritual growth, spiritual maturity is the base camp from which the ascent of the mountain of holiness can begin in earnest."[47]

We believe that recapturing this biblical vision for forming communities of mature missionary disciples—a goal that is attainable by the grace of God—is an important step for the Church's mission in the twenty-first century.

CHAPTER 3

Discipleship Is a Process

The goal of this chapter is to show how formation in mature discipleship is a process that takes place over time. This process of becoming a Christian has stages. We want to briefly consider some of the ways this process has worked throughout the Church's history and then consider the particular circumstances that should inform the process of formation in missionary discipleship today.

We are an impatient people living in an instant-gratification world. How quickly we can become frustrated when our computer slows down or when we're on hold for more than a couple of minutes with the customer service rep! We've grown accustomed to getting what we want, when we want it, at the push of a button or the click of a mouse. Amazon and eBay compete for our online business by promising next-day delivery, because they know that we will pay to avoid the wait.

In our evangelistic efforts, it's easy for us to adopt this same impatient attitude. We sense the urgency to do something to address the crisis as so many young people fall away from the faith, and we look for the quick fix. We can think, "All we need to do is bring in this speaker or promote this program or that approach, and our problems will be solved. We will reverse the present course."

Pope Benedict XVI warned us against this approach. We must avoid, he said,

> the temptation of impatience, the temptation of immediately finding the great success, in finding large numbers. But this is not God's way. . . .
>
> . . . [The] New Evangelization cannot mean: immediately attracting the large masses that have distanced themselves from the Church by using new and more refined methods.

Rather, he proposes that the "new evangelization must surrender to the mystery of the grain of mustard seed and not be so pretentious as to believe to immediately produce a large tree."[48]

Certainly we want to do all that we can to reach as many as we can, but we need to make sure that we are bearing "fruit that will last" (John 15:16). If our evaluation of the current situation is correct—namely, that we have lost the Christian foundation of our culture—then our undertaking is indeed daunting. It involves nothing less than advancing a culture, that is, a Christian way of living, that is counter to the prevailing popular culture. There can be no shortcuts. We need to be wise builders. Our task requires fundamental and comprehensive solutions.

Many in the Church today think about ministry and mission mainly as planning and participating in activities and programs. The approach is often to add new programs and activities under the banner of the New Evangelization. Sometimes we develop initiatives that have an evangelizing component to them, such as retreats in which we proclaim the gospel and call people to conversion. Or we start evangelistically oriented Bible studies or small groups. These are certainly steps forward. Often, though, we merely rename an existing program and call it evangelistic. What was formerly the faith formation program is now the New Evangelization program or the missionary discipleship program.

In the archdiocese to which I (Gordy) belong, some of our parishes are making an effort to respond to the call to evangelize. They're using a program that trains parishioners to go door-to-door, reaching out to inactive Catholics within the parish boundaries. On a few occasions, I have been invited to one of these parishes to help parishioners understand the basics of relational evangelization and how to prepare a personal testimony of their own faith journey.

The first time a parish leader explained this door-to-door program to me, I asked an obvious follow-up question: "So after you go out and meet these people in their homes and engage them in conversation about faith, what's next?" The leader told me that they equipped these evangelizers with a list of Mass times and had them encourage inactive parishioners to return to Sunday Mass.

It's good to train parishioners to reach out personally to their lapsed Catholic neighbors, but I wondered whether simply inviting them to return to Sunday Mass was an effective strategy. Even if someone does respond positively to the invitation and shows up at 10:00 a.m. Mass the next Sunday, it's unlikely that this will be enough to help them become a missionary disciple. This approach falls short because it fails to understand evangelization as a comprehensive process, a journey of several stages with mature discipleship as its goal.

Improving various elements of our Church life and programs is a seriously inadequate approach to our present situation. The Church needs to become, at every level, an evangelizing "community of missionary disciples," as Pope Francis says.[49] If we are going to achieve the goal of deep conversion and mature discipleship, then we need to move from an approach to ministry that is mainly activity, event, and program-centered to one that is relationship-centered, process-oriented, and goal-driven.

Activities, events, and programs are most effective when they take place in relationship to a process founded in authentic community and aimed at certain goals. We need to engage people relationally, call them to life-changing and integral conversion, form them to be mature disciples, and envision, equip, and send them on lifelong mission. All of this needs to take place in the context of a living Christian community. Let's unpack in greater detail the elements of this approach.

When Is Someone a Christian?

If the goal of evangelization and discipleship is to help someone become a Christian, it is important to be clear about what it means to be a Christian. As Catholics, our first inclination is to say that someone becomes a Christian when they are baptized. Broadly speaking, that is correct. The *Catechism* teaches:

> Holy Baptism is the basis of the whole Christian life, the gateway to life in the Spirit (*vitae spiritualis ianua*), and the door which gives access to the other sacraments. Through Baptism we are freed from sin and reborn as sons of God; we become members of Christ, are incorporated into the Church and made sharers in her mission. (1213)

A baptized person experiences the effects of the gift of salvation offered through the suffering, death, and resurrection of Jesus Christ. The baptized infant is freed from original sin, united with Christ, and incorporated into his body, the Church. This child is certainly a Christian. Many of those we evangelize as adults have already been baptized as infants and hence are Christians. Given this reality, how we can say that we are called to evangelize those who are already baptized and therefore are already Christians?

The point is, there is more to becoming a Christian than simply being baptized. Many in the Church now speak of the Sacrament of Confirmation as the moment when those baptized as infants complete the Sacrament of Baptism through their own assent of faith. But that doesn't always—or even often—happen.

I (Gordy) didn't make that assent of faith until I was nineteen, many years *after* my Confirmation. That conversion moment as a young man was an important step in my becoming a Christian. Others experience conversion while praying what is known as the sinner's prayer: acknowledging their sins, asking forgiveness, proclaiming faith in Jesus' death and resurrection, entrusting themselves to him, and choosing to follow him as Lord and Savior. Praying such a prayer can be an important moment in the process of becoming a Christian.

There are multiple ways we can understand the phrase "becoming a Christian." We can speak of becoming a Christian in an essential sense: that is, in receiving Baptism, one becomes a Christian. We can also speak of becoming a Christian in a full or integral sense. This is what we see when we consider the biblical testimony and the experience of the early Church: to become a Christian was to become a disciple of Jesus Christ, living entirely for God through the power of the Holy Spirit.

In short, in order to be a Christian, a person must be baptized. In order to be a Christian in a full or integral sense, however, other elements ought to be present. These include, among other things, an act of faith, repentance from sin, instruction, and being joined to a Christian community.

It is important to understand that Baptism is necessary in order to become a Christian. But in terms of our work in the New Evangelization, it's critical that we focus on the process of becoming a Christian in an *integral* sense.

A Note on Terminology

Before we turn our attention to identifying the elements that are integral to the process of becoming a Christian, it will help to step back and consider what we mean when we use the terms "evangelization" and "discipleship." "Evangelization" and "discipleship" refer to what followers of Jesus Christ do to help someone become a Christian and grow toward maturity. Both terms can be used to refer to the whole process of becoming a Christian.

Pope Paul VI proposed that evangelization is a "complex process made up of varied elements: the renewal of humanity, witness, explicit proclamation, inner adherence, entry into the community, acceptance of signs, apostolic initiative" (Evangelii Nuntiandi, 24). He suggests that the process is complete when the one evangelized becomes an evangelizer.

Here lies the test of truth, the touchstone of evangelization: it is unthinkable that a person should accept the Word and give himself to the kingdom without becoming a person who bears witness to it and proclaims it in his turn. (Evangelii Nuntiandi, 24)

Likewise, we can use the term "discipleship" to describe the whole process of becoming a Christian. When Jesus commissions the apostles to "go . . . and make disciples of all nations" (Matthew 28:19), he is calling them to engage in the entire evangelistic and formative process. The commission instructs them to "baptize" and "teach," but the complete process is implicit in the injunction to wait "until you are clothed with power from on high" (Luke 24:49). Jesus is of course referring to the Holy Spirit, who will be poured out on the feast of Pentecost to equip them for the task.

We can also use both terms to refer to an element of the process. Etymologically, "to evangelize" means to proclaim or announce good news. The angels evangelize when they announce the good news of Jesus' birth. John the Baptist evangelizes when *he calls the crowds to prepare for the kingdom of God. Jesus evangelizes at the synagogue in Nazareth, when he announces that the day of the Lord is at hand. When Peter stands up and preaches the gospel on the feast of Pentecost, he is evangelizing. Evangelization, understood as proclaiming the gospel, is one element in the evangelistic process.*

As with "evangelization," "discipleship" can also refer to a particular aspect of the evangelistic process, one that concerns growth to Christian maturity. A disciple is not simply one who decides to follow Jesus but the one who continues on in Christ and learns a way of life. "If you continue in my word," Jesus says, "you are truly my disciples" (John 8:31). The followers of Jesus entered into a process of discipleship by devoting themselves to him, following after him, and learning a way of life from him over the three years of his public ministry.

We will use "evangelization" and "discipleship" interchangeably to refer to the process of becoming a mature Christian.

The Process of Becoming a Christian

From the time of the apostles, becoming a Christian has been accomplished by a journey and initiation in several stages. This journey can be covered rapidly or slowly, but certain essential elements will always have to be present: proclamation of the Word, acceptance of the Gospel entailing conversion, profession of faith, Baptism itself, the outpouring of the Holy Spirit, and admission to Eucharistic communion.

This initiation has varied greatly through the centuries according to circumstances. (*Catechism*, 1229–1230)

One does not become a fully converted and mature disciple in a moment or through a singular experience. Becoming a Christian involves a process—that is, a series of actions or steps that produce change and lead toward a particular end or goal. The *Catechism* describes this process as both a "journey" and an "initiation" (1229).

"Journey" conveys the idea that we are traveling toward some destination, while "initiation" implies that we are becoming a member of something. Our task of forming missionary disciples requires us to be clear both about the goal for which we aim and the elements and dynamics that lead to that goal. Through the Church's history, the process of becoming a Christian has taken various forms while maintaining certain essential elements. Our task, we remember, is "scrutinizing the signs of the times," so as to effectively help people become Christian disciples in our time.[50]

We will look at three expressions of Christian initiations in the history of the Church, identify in them the common essential elements in the process of becoming a Christian, and consider how the historical and cultural context influenced their application. The three distinctive forms of the process of becoming a Christian that we will study are (1) the biblical form as described in Acts 2, (2) the catechumenate from the patristic era, and (3) the form that evolved in Christendom. We will conclude by applying what we learn to our current situation.

Evangelization in Acts 2

Let us begin by considering the process and elements of evangelization during the first days of the Church. The second chapter of the Acts of the Apostles gives us the first recorded account of evangelization following the Great Commission and Jesus' ascension. We are most familiar with the Pentecost event described in this chapter, but the chapter as a whole presents the evangelistic process. All the elements in the process of becoming a Christian are present here, flowing from the Pentecost event.

"When the day of Pentecost had come, they were all together in one place" (Acts 2:1). This short verse at the beginning of the Pentecost story is significant; we should not pass over it too quickly. Before they proclaim the gospel, the followers of Jesus are together as a community of disciples. It is in and through this community that the evangelistic process originates and unfolds. The disciples gathered in community are a primary and initial witness of the gospel.

Jesus demonstrated the importance of this communal witness at the Last Supper, when he prayed for his disciples: "That they may be one even as we are one, . . . so that the world may know that [you have] sent me" (John 17:22, 23). Jesus says that others may come to know the gospel when they see the Christian community living in unity. There is a vital connection between *communion* and *mission*.

John Paul II described the relationship between communion and mission this way:

Communion and mission are profoundly connected with each other, they interpenetrate and mutually imply each other, to the point that *communion represents both the source and the fruit of mission: communion gives rise to mission and mission is accomplished in communion.* It is always the one and the same Spirit who calls together and unifies the Church and sends her to preach the Gospel "to the ends of the earth" (Acts 1:8).[51]

The message of the gospel is that Christ's death and resurrection make it possible for us to live once again as we were created to live, in communion with God and one another. The aim of the evangelistic process is a life lived in love of God and neighbor. The Christian community, living in relationship with God and unity with one another, is both a means of advancing the gospel and its goal. In short, mission flows out of communion. The gospel message that we proclaim in mission is the message of communion, and mission finds its completion and fulfillment in communion.

John the Evangelist expresses it this way: "That which we have seen and heard we proclaim also to you, so that you may have fellowship with us; and our fellowship is with the Father and with his Son Jesus Christ" (1 John 1:3). The word "fellowship" is translated from the Greek *koinonia*, which in Latin is *communio*, from which we get the word "communion" that is used in the text from John Paul II above. We recognize the term *koinonia*, or "communion," in the opening greeting of the Mass: "The grace of our Lord Jesus Christ, and the love of God, and the *communion* of the Holy Spirit be with you all" (emphasis added).

The communion or fellowship of believers is, first of all, a spiritual communion. The communion we have with one another is our shared communion with the Father and the Son through the Holy Spirit. In Christ and through the Holy Spirit, we are called to "become partakers [*koinonoi*] of the divine nature" (2 Peter 1:4).

The communion of believers is also a sharing in a way of life and all aspects of life, from meals to money (see Acts 2:42), and a sharing (*koinonia*) in the gospel (see Philippians 1:5). The gift of the Holy Spirit that the believers received on the day of Pentecost is the source of the communion they share now in God and with one another.

The first response of the disciples to the outpouring of the Holy Spirit was the worship of God. All of them were filled with the Holy Spirit and began to speak in other languages, as the Spirit gave them the ability (see Acts 2:4). We see this connection between the outpouring of the Spirit and the worship of God throughout the Scriptures.[52] True worship, Jesus says, is in "spirit and truth":

> But the hour is coming, and now is, when the true worshipers will worship the Father in spirit and truth, for such the Father seeks to worship him. God is spirit, and those who worship him must worship in spirit and truth. (John 4:23-24)

When the community of believers, filled with the Spirit, worship God, they give witness to the presence and reality of God. We see this demonstrated in the Pentecost event. The Jews who were gathered in Jerusalem from all over the

Roman world were "amazed and perplexed" at what they were witnessing (Acts 2:12). This initial witness through the worship of God moved them, attracted them, and aroused their curiosity, such that they asked one another, "What does this mean?" (2:12).

The experience of a community of converted disciples gathered together and worshipping the Lord in song and prayer was instrumental in my (Gordy's) conversion. I wrote in chapter 1 about my first experience of a prayer meeting. I walked into a gathering of young men and women alive to the Spirit of God, full of faith and joy and singing and praying to the Lord with all their hearts. This community of believers—praying to God as if he actually existed, believing he would hear and receive their prayer—made God real to me.

I was struck immediately with a sense of the presence of God and his personal love for me, in a way I had never known before. It was that experience of love that began to open my mind and heart to the gospel. Those young people reached out to me with genuine interest and concern, and this initial experience of Christian hospitality and friendship also testified to the presence of God.

The Holy Spirit, poured out on the feast of Pentecost, is not only the source and inspiration for worship and communal life but is also the "principal agent of evangelization."[53] Wait until you are filled with the Holy Spirit, Jesus says— only then will you be my witnesses (see Acts 1:4, 8).

Pope Paul VI reminds us of this fundamental truth in his encyclical letter *Evangelii Nuntiandi*:

Evangelization will never be possible without the action of the Holy Spirit. . . .

Techniques of evangelization are good, but even the most advanced ones could not replace the gentle action of the Spirit. The most perfect preparation of the evangelizer has no effect without the Holy Spirit. Without the Holy Spirit the most convincing dialectic has no power over the heart of man.[54]

Evangelization is a spiritual work. Unless the Holy Spirit anoints our preaching, moves the hearts of the hearers to faith, and gives help for Christian growth, there is no effective evangelization. And so as the story of Pentecost unfolds, we witness Peter, "filled with the Holy Spirit" (Acts 2:4) beginning to preach to the people gathered in Jerusalem for the feast (2:14).

The preaching of the gospel is an essential element in the evangelistic process. As St. Paul says,

But how are they to call on one in whom they have not believed? And how are they to believe in one of whom they have never heard? And how are they to hear without someone to proclaim him? (Romans 10:14, NRSVCE)

The New Testament uses two related Greek words to describe this kind of preaching: *kerygma* and *kerusso*. We are perhaps more familiar with the noun *kerygma* (the proclamation of the gospel), as it has become a popular term today. But the New Testament uses the verb *kerusso* (to proclaim the gospel) more frequently.

The *kerygma* is the proclamation of the gospel message concerning the salvation offered to all through the paschal mystery, the death and resurrection of Jesus Christ. Peter's speech in Acts represents the first expression of the *kerygma*:

> You that are Israelites, listen to what I have to say: Jesus of Nazareth, a man attested to you by God with deeds of power, wonders, and signs that God did through him among you, as you yourselves know— this man, handed over to you according to the definite plan and foreknowledge of God, you crucified and killed by the hands of those outside the law. But God raised him up, having freed him from death, because it was impossible for him to be held in its power. . . .
>
> Therefore let the entire house of Israel know with certainty that God has made him both Lord and Messiah, this Jesus whom you crucified. (Acts 2:22-24, 36, NRSVCE)

We see the *kerygma* take the form of brief formulas like this in other places in the New Testament, for example in Romans 10:9: "If you confess with your lips that Jesus is Lord and believe in your heart that God raised him from the dead, you will be saved."

Pope Paul VI describes the *kerygma* and its place in evangelization in this way:

> Evangelization will also always contain—as the foundation, center, and at the same time, summit of its dynamism—a clear proclamation that, in Jesus Christ, the Son of God made man, who died and rose from the dead, salvation is offered to all men, as a gift of God's grace and mercy.[55]

The *kerygma* is more than simply communicating the content of a message; the preaching of the *kerygma* has a certain dynamism. *Kerygma* is the announcement of the basic gospel message, "Jesus is Lord," in the power of the Spirit, in a way that stirs the heart and awakens faith. When Peter stands to speak on Pentecost, his preaching has an authority that astonishes, amazes, and perplexes his hearers. They are moved to make a response: "Now when they heard this, they were cut to the heart" (Acts 2:37).

Paul VI speaks of the "hidden energy of the Good News, which is able to have a powerful effect on man's conscience."[56] This is precisely what we see in the Letter to the Hebrews:

> The word of God is living and active, sharper than any two-edged sword, piercing until it divides soul from spirit, joints from marrow; it is able to judge the thoughts and intentions of the heart. And before him no creature is hidden, but all are naked and laid bare to the eyes of the one to whom we must render an account. (4:12-13, NRSVCE)

The gospel, proclaimed in the power of the Holy Spirit, moves hearts and invites a response. The gospel requires a response in order to have its effect in our lives. It must be received. That which God has accomplished for us in Christ does not adhere to us automatically but requires our acceptance.

We see this demonstrated in the Pentecost event. The Jews who heard the preaching of Peter asked Peter and the other apostles, "Brothers, what should we do?" Peter replied, "*Repent,* and be *baptized* every one of you in the name of

Jesus Christ so that your sins may be forgiven; and you will receive the gift of the Holy Spirit" (Acts 2:37, 38, NRSVCE; emphasis added).

Repenting from sin and then being baptized are the way to receive and enter into the new relationship with God and his body, the Church. The New Testament also identifies faith as a necessary response to the gospel. Let's take a look at the biblical meanings of those three terms: faith, repentance, and Baptism.

Faith

Though not explicit in Peter's response, the New Testament is clear that faith must accompany repentance and Baptism. In Acts 16, we find Paul and Silas imprisoned in a Philippian jail for preaching the gospel. During the night, while Paul and Silas are singing hymns, there is an earthquake, the prison doors fly open, and all the prisoners' chains are loosened. The jailer, upon witnessing these events, cries out in the same way as the Jews in Acts 2, "Sirs, what must I do to be saved?" Paul and Silas respond, "*Believe* on the Lord Jesus, and you will be saved" (Acts 16:30, 31, NRSVCE; emphasis added).

Belief is also identified as the one condition for receiving salvation in the well-known expression of the *kerygma* in John's Gospel: "For God so loved the world that he gave his only Son, so that everyone who believes in him may not perish but may have eternal life" (3:16, NRSVCE). These are just two of many New Testament references that speak of faith as the proper response to the gospel.

Faith, or belief, is often commonly understood as intellectual assent to true propositions. I have faith if I believe that what I recite in the Creed is true. I have faith if I believe that what is proclaimed in the gospel is true. I have faith if I believe that Jesus is the Son of God, that he became man, that he suffered, died, and rose again.

Intellectual assent is certainly a dimension of an act of faith, but the biblical meaning of faith has a much deeper sense. The Greek word *pistis,* most often translated as "faith," appears over 240 times in the New Testament. It has several meanings—all related to faith—including loyalty, faithfulness, and firm conviction or belief. Its most common meaning, however, connotes trust or confidence.

In this sense, *pistis* is a relational word. St. Paul writes to Timothy, "I *know* the one in whom I have *put my trust*, and I am *sure* that he is able to guard until that day what I have *entrusted* to him" (2 Timothy 1:12, NRSVCE; emphasis added).

Our response of faith to the gospel means that we entrust ourselves and our lives to Jesus Christ, the Son of God. In the act of faith, there is a transfer of our loyalty and trust from ourselves or other things to the Lord God. That trust is total. It involves the commitment of our very lives. Faith involves knowing and having a relationship with the Lord and, on the basis and experience of this relationship, offering our whole lives to him.

In our evangelistic work, we often use the image of the throne in our hearts to communicate the type of surrender to God that takes place in this act of faith. The throne represents the reality to which our life is directed. Who sits on the throne of my life? Who is Lord or king of my life? Prior to conversion, we—or other "idols" in our lives—may occupy that central place on the throne. In the act of faith, we relinquish that place to God.

The *Catechism* describes the personal nature and total surrender of faith in this way:

> Faith is first of all a personal adherence of man to God. At the same time, and inseparably, it is a *free assent to the whole truth that God has revealed.* As personal adherence to God and assent to his truth, Christian faith differs from our faith in any human person. It is right and just to entrust oneself wholly to God and to believe absolutely what he says. It would be futile and false to place such faith in a creature (Cf. Jeremiah 17:5-6; Psalm 40:5; 146:3-4). (150)
>
> *By faith*, man completely submits his intellect and his will to God. With his whole being man gives his assent to God the revealer. (143)

Repentance

Reception of the gospel requires repentance along with faith. And as faith can be construed as mere intellectual assent, there can be a tendency to understand repentance as only the sorrow or sadness we have because of our sins.

The Greek word for repentance in the New Testament is *metanoia,* and it literally means "a change of mind." Repentance, then, is an objective, fundamental decision to turn away from or repudiate a way of living that is incompatible with a relationship with God. This involves much more than feeling bad for our sins. It is a recognition that certain actions and lifestyles are incompatible with a relationship with this new life in Christ to which he calls us.

Repentance is closely related to faith because it involves a transformative change of heart, a conversion. If faith is a turning *toward* the Lord in trust, surrender, and commitment, repentance is a turning *away* from what is contrary to faith. This involves a reorientation of one's life, sometimes a radical one.

Baptism

Responding to the gospel also requires Baptism. When Jesus commissioned the apostles to "go . . . and and make disciples of all nations," he established Baptism as a condition for fulfilling this commission: "baptizing them in the name of the Father and the Son and the Holy Spirit" (Matthew 28:19). When Jesus spoke to Nicodemus about how to enter the kingdom of God, he named Baptism as the condition: it is necessary to be "born of water and the Spirit" (John 3:5). Jesus demonstrated the importance of Baptism by submitting to it himself (see *Catechism*, 1147–1151).

The Church would eventually articulate a more developed sacramental theology and identify Baptism, Confirmation, and the Eucharist as sacraments of initiation. We see nascent forms of these sacraments represented in the Acts of the Apostles and connected to the evangelistic process. Baptism and Confirmation were indistinguishable at that time (see Acts 2:38, for example).

Baptism is the place where the saving action of God and the human response to that saving action meet. They make present for us the salvific work of Jesus Christ. The *kerygma* and the response of faith are the preconditions for Baptism and the forgiveness of sins, the new birth, and the gift of the Spirit. Faith, repentance, forgiveness of sins, and the outpouring of the Holy Spirit are the saving graces given when people submit to Baptism. The Eucharist is present in the concluding verses of Acts 2:42: "They devoted themselves to the apostles' teaching and fellowship, to the breaking of bread and the prayers."

In the Acts account, faith, repentance, and the reception of Baptism and the other sacraments of initiation together constitute the moment of conversion in the process of becoming a Christian. This conversion is the beginning of the Christian life and the way of discipleship. The experience of conversion is not, however, a singular event. The Christian life is marked by ongoing conversion, as God's grace brings us through the process of Christian growth and maturity.

The Pentecost event concludes as follows:

> So those who received his word were baptized, and there were added that day about three thousand souls. And they devoted themselves to the apostles' teaching and fellowship, to the breaking of bread and the prayers. (Acts 2:41-42)

The process of integral conversion and formation continues through life in the Christian community, growth in the life of prayer, the sacramental life, and instruction.

Jesus' injunction in the Great Commission, "[Teach] them to observe all that I have commanded you" (Matthew 28:20), suggests an ongoing process in the making of disciples. Paul's ministry entails both an unwavering commitment to the proclamation of the gospel and the forming of Christian communities, wherein believers are brought to maturity. Within these communities, Paul identifies those who are not yet spiritually mature (see 1 Corinthians 3:1-2; Galatians 4:19), and much of the writing in the New Testament epistles contains instruction aimed at maturity. Becoming a mature disciple in the New Testament requires learning to live in Christian love in community, putting off the ways of the flesh and living a life in the Spirit, embracing a deeper understanding of Christian truth, and growing in Christian virtue.

The Catechumenate in the Early Church

In the first centuries of the Church, Christian initiation saw considerable development.

> A long period of *catechumenate* included a series of preparatory rites, which were liturgical landmarks along the path of catechumenal preparation and culminated in the celebration of the sacraments of Christian initiation. (*Catechism*, 1230; emphasis in original)

The early Church made significant strides in developing a process for helping someone become a Christian. The approach that emerged became known as the catechumenate.

There is not a fixed and universal expression of the catechumenate process from the early Church. This was a period in Church history that was marked by significant growth and change in various places and cultures, within which various forms of the catechumenate developed. We can, however, identify some trends and common elements.

What was the impetus behind the development of the catechumenate? In the Book of Acts, the experience of becoming a Christian seems almost immediate—"And the Lord added to their number day by day those who were being saved" (2:47). The catechumenate, however, was an intense and focused process that occurred over several years. Most notably, it was a move away from proclaiming the Christian gospel mainly to Jews and toward evangelizing Gentiles.

The followers of Jesus first proclaimed the gospel to the Jews, and they built on the foundation of the old covenant, which the gospel fulfills. The Jews had many of the basics of Christian life already in place, including the moral teaching of the Ten Commandments, a regular pattern of prayer based on the psalms, a strong community life and communal identity, the Old Testament Scriptures, and belief in the one true God. Additionally, the Jewish way of life was counter to the broader culture. When Jews became followers of Jesus, they didn't need to make radical changes in their pattern of life.

The situation was different when the disciples began to proclaim the gospel to pagan Gentiles. Pagans, lacking the robust foundation enjoyed by the Jews, required much more formation in order to learn and live the Christian way of life. To address this need, the Church developed a process to help newly converted pagans move, over time, to full, integral conversion and mature discipleship.

We find records of the catechumenate in some of the post-biblical and patristic writings. We notice immediately when we study these accounts that Baptism and the other sacraments of initiation are received at the end of the evangelistic process. This seems to be a departure from the New Testament norm and is certainly different from today, when infant Baptism is the norm and consequently received as the first experience in the evangelistic process. If Baptism is received at the end of the catechumenate process, it cannot be the precondition or even the simultaneous condition for the experience of elements of conversion.

The Apostolic Tradition of Hippolytus is one of the earliest postbiblical accounts of the life of the Christian Church. Written between the years 200 and 225, it describes a lengthy, substantial process for bringing a person fully into the faith and the Christian way of life. *The Apostolic Tradition* seems to indicate that newcomers to the faith, early in the process of engaging with Christianity, had some experience of conversion. "New converts to the faith, who are to be admitted as hearers of the word, shall first be brought to the teachers before the people assemble. And they shall be examined as to their reason for embracing the faith."[57] These candidates being considered for admission to be hearers of the word were already described as "converts to the faith."

We see something similar in another early account of the catechumenate, in the *Didascalia Apostolorum*:

> When the heathen desire and promise to repent, saying "We believe," we receive them into the congregation so that they may hear the word, but do not receive them into communion until they receive the seal and are fully initiated.[58]

We can assume then that these new people had heard the gospel and had an encounter with Christ. They responded with faith and repentance, and they would commit to a lengthy period of formation in preparation for Baptism and full communion with the body of believers. We can presume as well that these candidates had some relationship with members of the Christian community, who bore witness on their behalf to the authenticity of this initial faith. This all occurred apart from the sacraments of initiation.

According to *The Apostolic Tradition,* those who were found ready then entered into a formation and discipleship period of three years.[59] During this time, they were allowed to remain in the Eucharistic assembly until the Eucharistic Prayer, at which time they left to receive their formation. The emphasis in this initial formation was moral rather than doctrinal. The aim was to help a person living in a pagan culture experience the growth that would enable them to fully live the Christian life. This involved learning about the Scriptures and personal and communal prayer as well as growing in the moral life through learning and living the commandments. Growth in virtue was a clear goal.

The *Didache* is one of the Church's earliest catechetical documents, most likely written before the year AD 100. The *Didache* prioritizes the need to form new Christians in the moral life, presenting the doctrine of the "Two Ways," one of which leads to life and the other to death. The way to life involves following the greatest commandment—to love God with your whole heart, mind, and soul, as Jesus preached—and growing in virtue. Teaching on the way to death warns against vices and practices contrary to the Christian life: "adulteries, lusts, fornications, thefts, idolatries, magic arts, . . . deceit, arrogance, malice, stubbornness, greed, foul speech, jealousy, audacity, pride, boastfulness."[60]

These early Christian writings also consider sexual practices. Those who were not married should abstain from fornication, for example, and those married are to be faithful to one spouse.[61]

Catechumens were expected to enter into and live the life of the Christian community. As the process drew toward completion, formation became more intense. It's striking to see the attention given to praying with and exorcising the candidates *daily* until the day of Baptism. The candidates were examined as to "whether they have lived honorably while catechumens, whether they honored the widows, whether they visited the sick, and whether they have done every good work."[62] Early Christian initiations gave significant attention to moral and behavioral formation. Catechumens were expected not only to have experienced some conversion but also to be following Christian practices.

This period of intense formation concluded as the candidates received the sacraments of initiation and entered into the full life of the community. Baptism, Confirmation, and the Eucharist were received in one event.

Christian Initiations from Constantine to the Modern Era

It is well beyond the scope of this book to give an in-depth presentation of the process of becoming a Christian as it evolved in the Western Church over fifteen hundred years. We will paint with very broad strokes.

The conversion of the Emperor Constantine in the early 300s and the Edict of Milan, which permanently established religious tolerance for Christianity, marked the beginning of a significant shift in the way the Church functioned in relationship to the broader culture. Initially, Christianity consisted of small, close-knit communities leading a life often counter to the broader culture. Over the succeeding early centuries of the Church, as Christianity became the dominant religion of the Roman Empire, large numbers of people sought entrance into the Church. The ability of the Christian community to form this flood of converts in the Christian way of life became seriously strained, and the catechumenate process was watered down.

Social realities, along with theological developments regarding the doctrine of original sin and sanctifying grace given in Baptism, gave increase to the practice of infant Baptism. A catechumenate process characterized by an intense period of conversion and formation as a prerequisite for Baptism and full entry into the Church disappeared over time. The result was that a person entered into a Christian way of life simply by being born into a Christian family and growing up in a Christian culture. Over the centuries, such a person would identify as Catholic by regularly participating in the life of the local parish; being formed in the moral life at home; receiving the Sacraments of the Eucharist and Confirmation, usually as a young person; and attending a Catholic school or at least a religious education program. The person would arrive at adulthood as a practicing Catholic, marry in the Church, and repeat the process with their own family. This way of becoming a Christian functioned with relative effectiveness within the Christian West, up until our modern age.

Becoming a Christian in the New Evangelization

We have already concluded that the process of Christian initiation that we have inherited from Christendom is seriously inadequate for our situation today. Pope Francis speaks of the massive change in our wider culture:

> Brothers and sisters, Christendom no longer exists! Today we are no longer the only ones who create culture, nor are we in the forefront or those most listened to. . . . We are no longer living in a Christian world, because faith—especially in Europe, but also in a large part of the West—is no longer an evident presupposition of social life; indeed, faith is often rejected, derided, marginalized and ridiculed.[63]

Christians cannot be formed through immersion in the culture because the culture is no longer Christian. We are called to evangelize people who are living in a culture that is increasingly different from and hostile to a Christian way of life.

The *Catechism* proposes,

> Where infant Baptism has become the form in which this sacrament is usually celebrated, it has become a single act encapsulating the preparatory stages of Christian initiation in a very abridged way. By its very nature infant Baptism requires a *post-baptismal catechumenate*. Not only is there a need for instruction after Baptism, but also for the necessary flowering of baptismal grace in personal growth. (1231, emphasis in original)

Infant Baptism by necessity requires experiences of conversion and formation after the fact. This conversion and formation are not occurring for most baptized-as-infants Christians. Catholics are arriving at young adulthood with a serious lack of basic Christian conversion and serious deficiencies in their Christian formation. Furthermore, there are increasing numbers of young people who have little or no exposure to Christianity. If we are to help them become fully converted and mature Christian disciples, we need to develop new approaches to Christian initiations.

Our situation today, according to Fr. Raniero Cantalamessa, resembles that of the apostolic period:

> Our situation is becoming more and more similar to that of the apostles. They were faced with a pre-Christian world to

evangelize; we have before us, at least to some extent and in certain quarters, a post-Christian world to re-evangelize. We need to return to their method by bringing anew to light "the sword of the Spirit," which is the announcement—in Spirit and power—of Christ who died for our sins and who rose for our justification (cf. Romans 4:25).[64]

If what Fr. Cantalamessa claims is true—namely, that the Church of today has characteristics similar to those in the early Church—then we propose that the process of evangelization employed by the early Church has application for us today.

Some years ago, my wife Teresa and I (Gordy) had the opportunity to travel in England on a canal boat. Centuries ago, canal boats moved products around the country on a series of man-made canals. Canals no longer serve this purpose, and so the canal boats have been converted into vacation boats equipped with a living room, kitchen, and bedroom. Teresa and I spent a week traveling the English countryside, and it was here that I had my first up-close experience of a lock-and-dam system.

At various points along the route, changes in elevation on the canals required locks and dams to raise the boat from one level of water to the next. At these points, I maneuvered our boat into the old wooden lock, closing the doors of the lock behind us. Then we opened the valve that allowed water to fill the lock. Slowly the boat would rise until the water in the lock reached the level of the canal ahead. We opened the forward doors of the lock and continued on our way.

Helping people become mature Christian disciples should work something like a lock-and-dam system. We encounter people at various places in their experience of Christian initiation and bring them gradually through the stages or "locks" that will raise them to the mature Christian high-water level. This approach is intentional. Every activity, event, or program is oriented toward a particular step in the process. Offering stand-alone activities and programs, even if they are excellent and well executed, won't accomplish this goal.

Pope Francis emphasizes the need for *process* in our present situation:

> We need to initiate processes and not just occupy spaces: "God manifests himself in historical revelation, in history. Time initiates processes and space crystalizes them. God is in history, in the processes. We must not focus on occupying the spaces where power is exercised, but rather on starting long-run historical processes. . . . This gives priority to actions that give birth to new historical dynamics. And it requires patience, waiting."[65]

Over the last forty years, we have developed a model that we have used effectively to bring thousands of university students and young adults to Christian maturity and lifelong discipleship. We have identified the following steps or stages: pre-evangelization, initial evangelization, conversion, formation, and lifelong mature discipleship. In recent years we have popularly defined our model as *reach, call, form,* and *send.*

It is not our intention to repeat the excellent work that outlines the steps of initial evangelization and conversion, such as Sherry Weddell explores in *Forming Intentional Disciples.* Our primary focus here is on bringing people to maturity as disciples. It is important, however, that we understand our particular focus in relationship to the whole. The early stages are necessary prerequisites, foundational for forming mature disciples. It is equally important to situate the entire process in the context of a community of missionary disciples.

Reach, Call, Form, and Send

In the remainder of this chapter, we will briefly highlight some priorities in initial evangelization (the *reach* stage) and conversion (the *call* stage), then develop central elements in the process of formation (the *form* stage). We conclude with a description of the community context at the center of the process, which culminates in sending.

Reach

Let's look at the first stage, *reach*. Simply put, we need to reach people if we are to make disciples. Reaching is the activity by which we initially encounter those who stand in need of the gospel. To reach them, we need to *go* to them. As Pope Francis says, "We 'cannot passively and calmly wait in our Church building;' we need to move 'from a pastoral ministry of mere conservation to a decidedly missionary pastoral ministry.'"[66]

Few university students are knocking on the doors of the campus ministry office or Newman Center, saying, "Help me grow in my faith." Many aren't even thinking about faith. If we're going to reach them, we need to engage them where they are, in the activities that make up their daily experience:

study, work, recreation, and socializing. The principal activity for the evangelizer or missionary in the reach stage is building relationships and forging friendships.

Pope Paul VI counseled,

> In the long run, is there any other way of handing on the Gospel than by transmitting to another person one's personal experience of faith? It must not happen that the pressing need to proclaim the Good News to the multitudes should cause us to forget this form of proclamation whereby an individual's personal conscience is reached and touched by an entirely unique word that he receives from someone else.[67]

Building relationships is central to our evangelistic work, not only because it is an effective means, which it is, but also because relationship is at the center of the gospel we proclaim. From the very beginning, God declared, "It is not good that the man should be alone" (Genesis 2:18). Yet loneliness is the main experience of many young people living in a culture that is profoundly individualistic and self-centered. In the words of St. Teresa of Calcutta,

> The greatest disease in the West today is not TB or leprosy; it is being unwanted, unloved, and uncared for. We can cure physical diseases with medicine, but the only cure for loneliness, despair, and hopelessness is love. There are many in the world who are dying for a piece of bread but there are many more dying for a little love. The poverty in the West is a different kind of poverty—it is not only a poverty of loneliness but also of spirituality. There's a hunger for love, as there is a hunger for God.[68]

There are no shortcuts to building authentic relationships. It's costly work. It involves investing ourselves in others, taking an interest in people, loving them, spending time with them, listening to them, and inviting them into our lives. In our university work, the first days and weeks of a new term are a critical time for reaching students and beginning to build relationships with them.

Our missionaries help with student move-in, are present at activity fairs, and daily host parties and events all around campus—with the simple goal of meeting other students. Some of our missionaries live in the dorms, giving them direct access to students in the midst of daily life. As we engage people in relationship, we invite them into our daily life and the activities of the communities we establish on campus: joining for dinner at a student formation house, attending a party, or participating in a sporting event.

As in the early Church, people are brought to the faith (or back to the faith) through the witness of Christians alive in the faith and through the life of an active Christian community. When students experience our communities of faith on university campuses, they are exposed to the quality of our relationships. There is something powerfully attractive about this witness.

Young people long for authentic relationships. When the Christian community is alive to the reality of Jesus Christ, then people discover Jesus in their relationships with Christians.

Call

The second stage of our process is the *call* to conversion. Keeping in mind that many people have already experienced some elements of conversion and Christian initiation, our aim here is to bring those we evangelize to full conversion. The faith that many of these students received in Baptism needs to come alive. The yes of faith expressed by parents and godparents needs to become an adult act of faith.

Fr. Cantalamessa stresses the priority of restoring the *kerygma*, found at the center of the testimony of Acts 2. He argues that the abundance of Christian doctrine today has the potential to obscure the proclamation of the gospel in the power of the Holy Spirit for those outside the Church. In our new state of affairs, it is vital that we restore the *kerygma* to a central place in our evangelization.

> So now, if we want to evangelize a secularized world, there is a choice to make. Where do we begin? From some place within that expanded wake or from its initial point? The immense wealth of doctrine and institutions can become a handicap if we are trying to present all of that to a person who has lost all contact with the Church and no longer knows who Jesus is.[69]

In the evangelistic stage that we identify as *call*, we create opportunities for an encounter with Jesus Christ in the power of the Holy Spirit, mainly through small groups and Bible studies focused on the basic gospel, larger evangelistic gatherings, and weekend retreats. Many students experience a conversion moment when they attend our Fan into Flame retreats, where they are offered an opportunity to welcome Jesus Christ into their lives in a deeper way. These community-centered and worship-filled retreats focus on the proclamation of the gospel, teaching, testimony, and the witness of the community.

During the central moment of the retreat, we invite participants to renew their baptismal promises, express a commitment to Jesus Christ as Lord, turn from sin, and receive prayer for an outpouring of the Holy Spirit. Paul, in his Second Letter to Timothy, exhorts Timothy to "fan into flame the gift of God" (that is, the Spirit) that was given to him when hands were laid upon him (1:6, ESV). During this prayer time, young people find the gift of the Spirit, given in the Sacraments of Baptism and Confirmation, reawakened and renewed in their lives.

Over the years, many students have referred to their experience of a Fan into Flame Retreat as a moment of deep conversion and a pivotal point in their becoming a disciple of Jesus Christ. It is a powerful testimony to the Lord's faithfulness, love, and mercy for his people that when we call upon him and ask for the outpouring of the Holy Spirit, he comes with an experience of his manifest presence. The joy, peace, and healing that people experience are life changing.

Yet these moments of conversion are really only the beginning of the process of becoming a mature disciple. As we have remarked, when faith is not *formed*, it can fade, like the seed that falls on shallow ground (see Mark 4:3-7, 14-19). We restate our conviction here that if our evangelistic work is going to produce fruit that will last, we need to be as serious about helping faith become mature as we are about fostering that initial conversion.

Form

The third stage of our process is *form*. This is, in a sense, the hard work of the New Evangelization. Just as the process of evangelization in Acts 2 can help us rediscover the integral aspects of full conversion, the model of the catechumenate in the early Church has much to offer on the process of helping people grow to Christian maturity. While bringing people to full or integral conversion can occur over a relatively short period of time, bringing people to mature discipleship cannot. In fact, the process of growing to maturity is never complete. Pope John Paul II wrote, "The gospel image of the vine and the branches reveals to us another fundamental aspect of the lay faithful's life and mission: *the call to growth and a continual process of maturation, of always bearing much fruit*."[70]

It helps to distinguish between ongoing growth throughout our lives and the particular formation and growth that occur at the beginning of the Christian life and, for our purposes here, during early adulthood, when one is getting established in life. For John Paul II, "the fundamental objective of the formation of the lay faithful is an ever-clearer discovery of one's vocation and the ever-greater willingness to live it so as to fulfil one's mission."[71] For this reason,

[I]n the life of each member of the lay faithful there are *particularly significant and decisive moments* for discerning God's call and embracing the mission entrusted by Him. Among these are the periods of *adolescence* and *young adulthood*.[72]

In order to effectively reach young people with the gospel and establish them as missionary disciples for life, the ideal strategy begins at adolescence and continues through the early period of establishing oneself in life. Within this age range—approximately thirteen to thirty—the university years are critical. This is when young people are living away from the direct authority and influence of their parents and in an environment often hostile to the Christian faith. They're making decisions that will have a significant impact on the rest of their lives.

Formation cannot simply be *information*. It's a mistake to assume that forming people in the Christian life means mainly teaching them doctrine or apologetics. Instruction is most certainly an essential element in formation; however, formation into Christian maturity is fundamentally about helping people conform their lives to the gospel, so that there is continuity between the faith they profess and the way they live.[73]

A Culture of Commitment

In many ways, the family serves as a model for how Christian formation occurs. In the family is where we learn what it means to be made in the image of God and to become like him in his way of love. It's the primary place of formation in the school of love.

We would not describe a family as a program or set of activities, though a family has those elements. Fundamentally, family is relational, defined by the relationships we have within the family. As the saying goes, you can choose your friends, but you can't choose your family. This is true. Nevertheless, a child can learn how to live well with others by living family life, day in and day out.

The formation process that we establish in our university and young-adult work has family-like elements to it. At the heart of the process is what we call the formation community. When those we are evangelizing have experienced integral conversion, we invite them into the formation community. They must make a commitment to be part of the formation community for a year and to participate in the various elements of community life.

These elements include (1) attending formation classes, (2) being in a men's or women's formation small group, (3) periodically meeting with an older brother or sister in the Lord who acts as a mentor, (4) praying with the formation community, and (5) being involved with mission and service. We will develop these elements more fully in the next chapter.

Without a commitment, formation won't happen. The commitment to faithfully participate is the foundation for fostering the family-life dynamic. By requiring young people to agree to this, we help them see the importance of making commitments if they are to grow as Christians. This call to commitment is a key responsibility for leaders if they are to establish effective formation programs and processes.

We live in a culture that is allergic to commitment. Young people in particular want to keep their options open and not be tied down, in case something "better" comes along. When we commit ourselves to the process—or more importantly, to the people in the formation community—we find that we press through difficult situations and grow through them.

Through the years, I (Gordy) have regularly found myself in situations in which there is one person who irritates me, someone I find difficult to love. Without commitment, I could simply move on from that relationship when the going gets tough. But sticking with the relationship expands my ability to love. Commitment is critical to Christian growth, helping us establish an environment or community of stable relationships.

It's no accident that family is a primary image for the Church in the New Testament. We are brothers and sisters in Christ, committed to one another. Our work in the New Evangelization requires that we build families of faith from which we can reach others with the love and mercy of God. Within our family-like formation process, we teach young people how to live the Christian life: how to pray, how to forgive, how to repair wrongdoing, how to use speech in a way that upbuilds and gives life, how to use time well, how to live in faith, how to be a servant, how to grow in virtue, how to be a good student, how to order sexual desire, how to discern vocation, and so on.

We also establish men's and women's formation houses near college campuses or within dorms, where missionaries and students live together. These households function within a broader formation community and include shared meals, common prayer, and a commitment to hospitality. Not only are the households centers of mission and evangelization where new people can be welcomed, but they're also centers where significant growth in maturity can occur.

Students often say that living for a season in a household with six to ten other men or women was one of their most difficult experiences but one of the most growth-filled. Also, the household experience can compensate for the basic human formation often lacking in the lives of young people who come from broken family situations. Formation happens when I learn to keep my room clean and get along with housemates.

The last stage of our process is *send*. And here we come full circle. Pope Paul VI says that the process of evangelization is only complete when the one evangelized becomes an evangelizer. We invite, call, and train students to become missionaries as students—and then for the rest of their lives.

The next two chapters will develop the structural elements and dynamics that are important parts of the formation process.

CHAPTER 4

Vehicles of Formation

The goal of this chapter is to describe the main vehicles we use in the formation of missionary disciples and to illustrate how they work in practice. There is a tendency, when pursuing discipleship formation, to latch on to one essential approach to do all the work. We have found the most effective process includes a set of interacting and complementary approaches, grounded in a community context and led by trained missionary disciples.

As we move to the topic of vehicles of formation, let's first review what we have already covered in our study of discipleship formation. First, we have shown the great need in our time for a community of mature missionary disciples (chapter 1). For the Church to flourish in our time, forming missionary disciples is essential.

Second, we have looked to Jesus to discover patterns for how we should go about forming disciples (chapter 2). Scripture presents us with foundational principles and patterns for raising up a generation of missionary disciples today.

Third, we have shown that discipleship formation is a process that unfolds in discreet stages (chapter 3). Recognizing and cooperating with these stages aids our efforts to accompany people on the path of discipleship.

Now we want to ask the question: "What are the main vehicles that carry the process of formation forward? What are the tools that will help us form others as disciples of Christ?"

When Jesus called his original disciples and they dropped their nets to follow him, they embarked on a season of training that prepared them to be the leaders of his people. Followers of Jesus today need such training too.

There is a tendency to latch on to one main vehicle and make this the mode of discipleship formation. Often this happens because one particular approach has worked really well for us, and so we make this our main approach. Or this happens because of limited resources: "We can't do everything, so we've decided to focus on this one strategy because we think we can achieve our goals with this."

For example, perhaps a Christian student organization uses one-to-one mentoring as the central approach to discipleship formation. Those who were personally mentored in turn mentor others in the same way. We give as we have received. In another discipleship model, however, the small discipleship group of three to five people functions as the single strategy for discipleship formation. Those who experience this intensive group formation form similar small groups. Although we believe that personal mentoring and small groups are indispensable to discipleship formation, in our experience they work best when they function in tandem with other approaches. It is wise not to put the full weight of discipleship formation on a single vehicle.

We have identified five main vehicles for discipleship formation:

1. meetings for common prayer,
2. formative teaching that leads people through the process of formation,
3. small discipleship groups,
4. personal mentoring, and
5. an active place in mission.

As we have seen, the context in which these flourish is a community in which people experience real friendship and grow together as disciples of Christ. Further, they take part in discipleship formation, not just programs, however valuable programs may be as instruments. In other words, the vehicles of formation flourish best in a community context and require trained leaders to help people grow as mature missionary disciples.

Complementary Vehicles

We envision a set of interacting, complementary vehicles. In order to get a sense of how they might function together, let's consider an ideal picture with all the vehicles in place and working well. In reality, one or more of these may be lacking or not functioning well: as with any labor in the Lord, there is always work to be done and room for improvement. But we have found that these five means of formation, together, genuinely work in real life; they have borne fruit in the lives of many missionary disciples.

1. Meetings for Common Prayer

Prayer is central to the Christian life, and helping people learn how to pray is an essential task of discipleship formation. Personal prayer is critical to the life of the disciple. We're concerned here, however, with prayer in common—that is, with meeting together for prayer.

What happens when we pray together with one voice? We are drawn into unity—the unity of the Father, Son, and Spirit and unity with each other. Prayer in common brings about this spiritual unity and functions as the center of our formation community. All other activities flow from this.

There are three main elements in our common times of prayer:

(1) praise and worship directed to God,
(2) listening for the word of the Lord to us, and
(3) praying for our own needs and the needs of the mission we share.

We begin by turning our minds and hearts together toward God in praise and worship. This centers us, taking our attention off ourselves and setting it on God. Human beings were created to give praise and worship to God, beginning now and continuing in eternity. As human beings in a fallen world, we are preoccupied with our own needs and desires—especially today, with the intense focus on the individual and the needs of the individual. Common prayer helps heals this self-oriented posture by turning us toward the source of our lives. It calls us to give glory to the Lord God and to do this together.

Contemporary Christian worship has been criticized for being at times "me-centered" and deliberately stirring up and manipulating the emotions. In view of this tendency (which is real), we aim in our common prayer to carry out a Copernican revolution that decenters us and recenters our attention on God. The music we use, therefore, is God-centered, and it expresses the truths of the faith. It is by turning our gaze toward the Lord God that we find true freedom and life: "He is the source of your life" (1 Corinthians 1:30).

When people come together and joyfully lift their hearts and voices to God in song and prayer, God is glorified, and people are set free in his presence:

> For a day in thy courts is better
> than a thousand elsewhere. (Psalm 84:10)

From this posture of actively setting our minds and hearts on God, we enter the second part of common prayer, in which we open ourselves to hear God's word to us. This may come through a conviction of the heart that a person shares with the whole group, perhaps something they learned in Bible study. Or it may come through a spiritual sense, such as what we see demonstrated in the Pentecost event (see Acts 2). God himself wishes to speak a message to us, so we may say out loud, "I believe God is saying to us . . ."

When Jesus met with his disciples, even after his resurrection, he spoke with them and to them—he conversed with them, together. He continues to do this, through the Holy Spirit, if we give him the opportunity.

This time of listening for the word of the Lord is also a time for training and apprenticeship. It gives people a safe place to hear God's word and to practice delivering what they hear in a way that helps the group. Many of these initial efforts lack polish and precision, but in the process, young disciples learn how to come before God, receive his word, and deliver that word for the common good.

Finally, we come before God in petition and with thanksgiving. We pray together for our own needs but especially with an eye to the common mission and the needs of others. To become a mature disciple means to move beyond praying only for my needs, asking God to bless my life and my projects; it means taking on the mind of Christ, becoming a coworker with him in his vineyard, seeking to cooperate with what he is doing in the world.

The prayer of thanksgiving accompanies our prayer of petition: "Have no anxiety about anything, but in everything by prayer and supplication with thanksgiving let your requests be made known to God" (Philippians 4:6). When we call upon God with thanksgiving, we reap the wonderful fruit of "the peace of God, which passes all understanding" (4:7).

In short, common prayer is a central vehicle for discipleship formation. It is a time when we come together as missionary disciples before God to give him praise, to hear his voice, and to call upon him for the needs of ourselves and the mission.[74]

2. Formative Teaching

Currently, many Christians are confused about the place of formative teaching in shaping disciples. We are well aware that Christian young people (and old people!) have been poorly formed in the faith; studies show that we just don't know our faith very well.[75] And so we grieve over our present crisis and speak about the desperate need for solid teaching in basic Christian truth.

Yet it seems that whenever a program begins to offer solid teaching, the opposite complaint arises: "People—especially young people—don't like to sit and listen to talks; they're not interested; they'll just go away." And so we move away from formative teaching and look for other ways to capture their attention.

Our own conviction is that we—as Christians seeking to become mature disciples—need to have our *minds* transformed: "Do not be conformed to this world but be transformed by the renewal of your mind" (Romans 12:2). Teaching plays a crucial and irreplaceable role in this transformation of mind. We cannot make significant progress in discipleship without regular sound teaching on the Christian life.

At the same time, teaching is not the whole of formation. And it's not as if teaching represents 90 percent or more of formation, with other things filling in the remainder. Formative teaching is an integral part of discipleship formation, but it needs to be embedded within other elements and applied in actual life.

How much teaching is helpful? When should people begin to receive teaching? At what point does teaching, however good, become counterproductive? When is it given in doses too large for people to handle?

We try to follow the basic wisdom outlined in the Book of Hebrews: the author speaks about beginning with "milk" and moving on to "solid food" (see 5:11-14). New Christians need sound teaching, but this works best when delivered in small packages laced with inspiration. For those who are growing in the Lord, they can and should learn to handle more weighty teaching about the faith, but even here we need a method, a pedagogy, that suits current generations. And crucially, people need space and time to apply the teaching they receive, or else the instruction will just pile up like notebooks on a desk.

Our experience is that when we prepare people well and inspire them to pursue their faith deeply, they respond with enthusiasm. They gladly engage in programs of formative teaching if they can see that this teaching is bearing fruit in their lives. This foundational teaching, in turn, anchors them in the truth and facilitates their growth as disciples of Christ.

In terms of frequency, we have found that formative teaching every two weeks provides a solid diet of spiritual nourishment that most people are able to digest. Some programs offer weekly teaching; others provide teaching once per month. Whatever the rhythm, the key is to offer teaching in a way that aligns with the process of discipleship and that helps people grow from stage to stage. For example, the first level of teaching should help anchor new Christians in basic Christian truth and practice. This includes topics such as

- who God is—Father, Son, and Spirit—and what he has done for us in Christ;
- growing in faith, hope, and love;
- responding in faith to the world, the flesh, and the devil;
- taking a daily time for prayer;
- prioritizing one's life to put Christ at the center; and
- seeing the value and importance of meeting with other Christians.

This basic teaching normally goes hand in hand with being part of a small group and receiving personal mentoring. In the small group, people can talk through their experiences and together apply the teaching they are receiving; with the personal mentor, people can receive counsel tailored to their personal needs. It is important to recognize that the goal is not simply to get the teaching done and "get people through it"; the goal is to help people genuinely receive and begin to live out the teaching. We need to resist the curricular approach to teaching, which concludes that the job is done just by virtue of giving the teaching. The program of formation is successful only when people effectively apply and live out the teaching.

The second level of formative teaching includes

- deeper understanding of the Lord God, who made all things and renews all things in Christ;

- instruction on personal relationships following biblical patterns of speech and relating;
- teaching on the gifts and fruits of the Spirit, with accompanying prayer;
- instruction on Christian sexuality and wisdom for relating together as men and women; and
- teaching on the place of emotions in the Christian life.

In general, formative teaching occurs over two to three years. It provides a kind of spine along which progress in discipleship can occur among people who are embedded within a community of disciples and who have time and space to apply the teaching. Seeing friends grow as disciples and living in an environment where people are applying the teaching really helps the teaching stick.

There is no need to hurry the process; nothing is gained by cramming lots of teaching into a short space. And while we should aim to provide formative teaching in a way that makes sense according to the pattern of how disciples grow, we will never have a system through which each individual goes as though on an assembly line. The process is never neat or simple; life is messy, and people progress according to their own capabilities and circumstances. Nevertheless, it is immensely helpful to have a path for people to follow and then to make the necessary adjustments to help individuals find their way, as unique individuals, toward mature missionary discipleship.

3. Small Discipleship Groups

For me (Dan), the path to discipleship really began when I joined my first small group. I was thrilled to be invited. I knew all the other young men in the group, I looked up to them (I was the youngest of them), and I genuinely looked forward to meeting with them every two weeks. The small group meeting became one of the highlights of my week.

Up until this point, I had been making strides—taking individual steps forward. But it was when I committed to being part of a regular small group that the integration of the various elements of discipleship began to happen for me.

Small groups have become a staple of discipleship formation, and rightly so. But there is often a large gap between the expectation of what a small group will provide and the reality of how the group actually functions. Why is this so?

First of all, an effective small group needs a clear focus and purpose. According to one model, the small group is a place to work on a topic or theme together: it is effectively a study group or Bible study. The group comes together primarily to pursue some common goal: working through the Bible, for example, or reading a book. These small groups have one great advantage: they have a focus, and it is relatively easy to lead the group through the study together. In one sense, small groups focused on study provide much of what often happens in the context of formative teaching. They are focused on giving regular spiritual food to the participants and helping them apply this in daily life.

According to another model, the small group is primarily a place to talk about what is happening in my personal life. It's a chance to open up and speak about things in my life within a protected, safe environment. Most people lack a context for speaking openly about their lives, and small groups offer chances to do this with other committed Christians. The group becomes primarily a place to share our lives and receive personal support in the context of friendship. The challenge of this approach is that it lacks a common outward purpose and can become dominated by people's problems and issues. It becomes problem-focused, often without an effective way to help people handle the problems that arise.

The model for small groups that we have adopted includes both of the above elements. The focus is on *the process of discipleship*, and the group is aimed at helping people progress as disciples of Jesus. What, then, is the typical anatomy of these small groups?

The first element is brief common prayer. This centers the group on God and provides an opportunity to learn to pray in a small environment. People begin to take responsibility in prayer for other people.

After prayer, the group is ready to begin its discussion. Sometimes the small group will have a thematic purpose: working through a Bible study or a topic, such as how to have an effective personal prayer time. But normally, the preponderance of the group's time is spent on the individuals' sharing about their lives, with the focus on the elements of discipleship that they are engaging. This is where the small group ties in with the program of formative teaching.

The group is focused, then, on taking positive strides as disciples, building on the teaching that everyone is receiving together. The small group also provides the occasion for the leader to give encouragement and counsel and for the other members (as they are able) to offer their own words of encouragement. An effective small group teaches people how to share their lives, how to listen to others, and how to offer helpful encouragement.

Crucial to effective small groups are leaders who are trained to lead them. The best prerequisite for leading a group is to have been an active member of a previous group. People learn how to lead by participating in small groups themselves.

But alongside this experience, we also give basic instruction to small group leaders about leading an effective group: how to bring focus to the group, how to ensure that all the members are participating, how to handle distractions and issues that arise, and when to refer someone to resources outside the group, such as when problems arise. In addition to this training for leading groups, it is important that small group leaders receive supervision and encouragement so that they can talk with an experienced trainer about how their groups are going.

Small groups are critical vehicles for discipleship formation, but they often falter or fail. To work well, they need a clear purpose, a consistent format, and effective leaders. When these are in place, small groups can and do bear abundant fruit. They are, in a sense, the lynchpin of the entire formation process, the "location" where the many elements of the process come together and can be applied.

4. Personal Mentoring

In his apostolic exhortation The Joy of the Gospel, Pope Francis offers this compact statement: "Missionary disciples accompany missionary disciples."[76] This phrase captures what we mean by personal mentoring as an important vehicle for forming mature missionary disciples. Alongside the other important vehicles, one-to-one mentoring provides a unique ingredient that truly accompanies the individual through the process of formation.

Yet this mentoring is one of the most difficult things to procure. It's not easy to find trained missionary disciples to accompany others on this path. So the role of mentoring—of accompaniment—often happens in an ad hoc way if it happens at all.

To gain a clear understanding of what we mean by personal mentoring, it helps to clear away two potential obstacles. First, personal mentoring is not the same as professional counseling. More and more people today need some form of professional counseling, and we want to have this avenue available for those who are traveling the road of discipleship, as they have need. But personal mentoring is different from counseling.

The personal mentor is a friend who accompanies another disciple on their common road. Those fulfilling this role should have basic instruction in what it entails, but they do not need professional training to function as personal mentors. Counseling is normally driven by the needs of the individual and is often problem based. Personal mentoring is focused on helping the individual appropriate and apply the elements in the process of discipleship formation. Simply put, mentoring means helping someone grow as a disciple of Jesus.

For Catholics, personal mentoring can also sound like an equivalent to spiritual direction. Spiritual direction is a time-honored practice in the Church whereby priests or lay-persons, trained to be spiritual directors, help individuals make spiritual progress and grow in their faith. There is some overlap between what happens in personal mentoring and spiritual direction, but there are also important distinctions.

Often the best spiritual directors are men and women who are deeply experienced in the spiritual life and can help people through difficult and dark terrain. To be an effective personal mentor, one only needs to be further ahead on the road of discipleship. Sometimes an older student can function as a friend and mentor to a younger student, helping that person make basic steps on the path of discipleship. In our experience, many of the Christian faithful can act as personal mentors and genuinely help people advance in the Lord.

What are the basic qualifications for being a personal mentor? First, the mentor must be a committed missionary disciple. As Pope Francis says, it is missionary disciples who can accompany and help form other missionary disciples. Second, mentors should have demonstrated stability and faithfulness in their own lives.

Third, a mentor should have the disposition to be with others, listen to them attentively, and be concerned for their good. Some people, unfortunately, seek Christian service as a way of working out something in their own lives. Mentors need to be focused on others, able to offer themselves and their encouragement freely for the good of others.

Fourth, it's best if mentors have experienced what it means to be mentored by another, but they should also receive basic instruction about what it means to mentor others, knowing what they are aiming for as well as being coached about the limits of their role.

Finally, mentors should have recourse to more experienced people, to whom they can go for help and counsel. One important role of the mentor is to know how to refer someone for the kind of help that goes beyond the normal vehicles (for example, for professional counseling, prayer for healing, spiritual direction, and so on).

In the process of formation, the personal mentor plays a key role in helping the individual navigate the road and work with the elements of formation. People may need more time to take certain steps; they may need extra help to get over a hurdle; they may benefit from richer spiritual food because the process is too slow for them.

How often should someone meet with a personal mentor? There is no fixed standard. We have found that meeting at least once per month is a helpful baseline during a season of active formation. Some people will benefit from more frequent meetings if this is possible.

Mentors are not independent agents. It's crucial that the mentor serve as part of the overall team doing formation. Things are likely to get off track if mentors follow their own agendas and ideas for what people might need. The various vehicles of formation need to work in tandem and in harmony. Those serving the formation process need to work together toward a common goal: helping people become mature missionary disciples of Christ.

5. An Active Place in Mission

Pope Francis offers strong encouragement for new disciples to be engaged in mission, right from the start:

> The new evangelization calls for personal involvement on the part of each of the baptized. Every Christian is challenged, here and now, to be actively engaged in evangelization; indeed, anyone who has truly experienced God's saving love does not need much time or lengthy training to go out and proclaim that love. Every Christian is a missionary to the extent that he or she has encountered the love of God in Christ Jesus: we no longer say that we are "disciples" and "missionaries," but rather that we are always "missionary disciples."[77]

There can be a temptation—for what seem like good reasons—to postpone missionary engagement until after someone is well formed as a disciple. While it makes sense to ensure that there is time and space for adequate formation, we have found that ongoing engagement in mission *right from the beginning* not only helps the mission grow but is a crucial part of discipleship formation itself.

As we saw in chapter 2, Jesus models this pattern for us. He called disciples to himself and began to train them personally. But right from the start, they followed him to the margins of his missionary work; he included them in ways they were capable of fulfilling. At the start, it seems, they mainly helped with practical matters and watched Jesus as he taught, preached, healed, and delivered people from spiritual bondage. Then Jesus began, step-by-step, to include them more fully, asking them to help supply the food for the multitude in the wilderness and having them distribute the bread that he had multiplied.

At a key point, Jesus gave a solemn charge to his followers (the Twelve and then the seventy) to go out *on their own* and do the things in mission that he had been doing (see Matthew 10:1-42; Luke 10:1-20). And they returned with testimonies of powerful works, rejoicing that they had been given a share in this mission.

Finally, as Jesus prepared to depart from the earth in his ascension, he charged the disciples to spread the gospel to the ends of the earth, with the Holy Spirit filling them, leading them, and directing them (see Acts 1:8).

New disciples serve the mission in two important ways. First, they contribute practically to missionary events and activities. This often involves preparing food, helping create publicity, setting up rooms and sound equipment, and so forth. But even more centrally, new disciples contribute to the mission by giving simple testimony to what God has done in their lives. They often have friends and acquaintances who are not Christians or at least not disciples. The freshness of their testimony can be a powerful tool for helping others hear and respond to the gospel.

These new disciples might not have the wisdom to counsel or mentor others. They may not be able to answer difficult questions about the faith. But through the simple account of their testimony to God's work in their lives, they provide an important element in the overall mission. As a result, they are often the most effective frontline evangelists.

What preparation does someone need to become mission ready? As Pope Francis points out, the people touched by Jesus in the Gospels did not need extensive instruction in order to *begin* witnessing to what Jesus had done for them:

> Let us look at those first disciples, who, immediately after encountering the gaze of Jesus, went forth to proclaim him joyfully: "We have found the Messiah!" (Jn 1:41). The Samaritan woman became a missionary immediately after speaking with Jesus and many Samaritans come to believe in him "because of the woman's testimony" (Jn 4:39). So too, Saint Paul, after his encounter with Jesus Christ, "immediately proclaimed Jesus."[78]

The first and most natural means of witnessing is to speak in our own words about what God has done. We have found that helping people practice giving their personal testimony is one of the most effective ways of initial formation in mission. By rehearsing their witness before others, they can receive input about what is helpful (and what is not), how to say things in a good way, and how to keep on track.

As people continue on the path of discipleship and learn more about their faith, they become increasingly equipped to answer questions and so to give an account "for the hope" that is in them, with gentleness and respect (1 Peter 3:15).

Our aim, as missionary disciples of Jesus, is to be always mission ready, able to respond to each situation with words and actions that bring the presence of Christ to others. The process of discipleship formation, therefore, should enlist people in mission, encouraging them to reach out to those around them and to take advantage of opportunities to make Jesus known and loved.

Community: The Context for Discipleship Formation

For me (Dan), formation as a disciple occurred in the midst of a living community of disciples. In fact, it was the broader student community that first welcomed me and gave me the vision for what it meant to be a disciple.

Like nearly all students beginning their college life, I was looking for friends. There is a deep instinct in all of us to find people we can be at home with; one of our greatest fears is simply being alone and having no one to spend time with. As a first-year college student, I quickly got to know the men on my dorm corridor and began doing things with them.

But it was my new Christian friends that I found most attractive. I was drawn to them, not only because of their faith but because of the quality of their relationships and the way that they welcomed me. Simply put, I was drawn by their goodness, expressed through their offers of friendship.

It didn't take me long to realize that these particular friends were together because they shared a strong faith in (and love for) Jesus. I was fine with that and, in some ways, glad for this emphasis, but it took me some time to warm up to the idea of following Jesus. My new friends were patient as well as welcoming.

Within two months, they invited me to a Life in the Spirit Seminar, which I readily attended. I found the teaching quite basic but was struck by the simple truth that God sought a relationship with me. I began to pray each day (for the first time in my life), and through the accompanying prayer of others, I experienced the clear presence of God in my life—an encounter with the person of Jesus through the power of the Spirit and a clear grasp of the love of God the Father for me. I experienced what Romans 8:16 describes: "The Spirit himself bearing witness with our spirit that we are children of God."

All this was quite powerful. It was clear to me that nothing could ever be the same. God had entered my life, and there was no going back.

As I said yes to God, my path of discipleship opened before me. All aspects of this process occurred within a community of other disciples who were walking beside me (and thankfully, *ahead* of me). I began to attend large meetings for common prayer; I was invited into a small discipleship group; I began to meet with a personal mentor; I set aside time for regular teaching on the basics of Christian discipleship; and I joined with others in a common mission to the students around us. The vehicles were hugely helpful, but the community context for these vehicles was equally important.

Creating—or better, *cultivating*—this community environment takes time. It means working with a few people to create the kind of environment in which others can be welcomed and discipleship breathed in. As Curtis Martin says, "Everything begins to change when a *culture* of missionary disciples is established."[79]

A discipleship culture is unlikely to come about by accident, by simply scheduling an event and having people turn up. It needs to be modeled by those who lead; it has to be taught and envisioned so that people can grasp the kind of culture we seek to have together. In other words, we need to experience this culture of community, but we also need an explicit vision for why we should embrace it and practical instruction for living this common way of life.[80]

In our experience, the most effective environments for discipleship include a combination of mixed environments—men and women together—and environments of men and women meeting separately. Meetings for common prayer, most social events, and much formative teaching happen best in mixed environments, but we also hold regular events for men or women where specific topics can be raised (sexuality, for example) and where relationships of brotherhood or sisterhood can be fostered. In particular, personal mentoring and small discipleship groups work best when they are "women with women" and "men with men."

Meeting separately as men or women, even on occasion and for special purposes, is countercultural today. Yet we believe such meetings are critical for healthy discipleship formation, especially among young people. These meetings help create and cultivate a culture of missionary discipleship in which personal sexual identity and healthy relationships between the sexes can flourish.

A reasonable question arises at this point: How can we create and cultivate a community environment when we don't have one to start with? How do we get there?

There is no substitute for seeing and experiencing how healthy communities work. Therefore, one of the most effective means of cultivating such environments is to invite your core group to visit a flourishing environment—over a weekend perhaps, visiting households or attending short-term "schools." Whether you are hoping to form a student group or a parish-based discipleship program, "live" experience of a real community environment can be immensely fruitful.

A second step is to consult with people who have formed such community environments. Invite them to visit (if possible) and help you implement basic steps with a core group. Though it may take time, forming a community environment—a culture—of missionary discipleship is enormously valuable and worth the effort. It is within such a community setting that the vehicles of formation thrive and bear fruit.

The Role of Trained Leaders

To conclude this chapter on the vehicles of formation, we think it is important to underline the ingredient that makes these vehicles effective and fruitful—namely, trained leaders who serve in unity under the leading of the Holy Spirit. A successful program of discipleship formation doesn't require supermen and superwomen to run it, but it does require solidly formed and trained leaders who are clear in their minds about what they are doing (that is, they are intentional) and zealous in Christ to serve others. To borrow again the phrase from Pope Francis, what we need are "missionary disciples" to lead others to become effective missionary disciples.

This means that we want our programs to multiply gifts of leadership as quickly as possible. While we don't want to throw people into the deep end of the pool when they cannot swim, it's better to give people a bit more than they can handle (rather than less) and allow the grace of God to work in them and bring about a fruitfulness that they never anticipated.

While still an undergraduate student, I (Dan) was invited to participate in a summer mission trip to the Philippines. The prospect of traveling across the world to serve in mission was in equal parts exhilarating and terrifying. After landing, I had a serious bout of anxiety about my abilities and wondered if I would be a failure. Why had we spent so much money to bring me across the world? What did I have to offer the people here? I was just learning what it meant to be a disciple myself.

With patient encouragement from our mission leader, I overcame these anxieties and jumped into the activities all around me. Things went surprisingly well. My first (ever) public speaking appearance happened on a weekend retreat in front of four hundred Filipinos. I can still recall walking up to the podium completely terrified, hoping I wouldn't freeze up in public. But the fifteen-minute meditation went fine, and gradually I learned to be at peace and to speak confidently in public.

The Church in our day is in great need of trained missionary disciples who can go out and witness to others. Just as Jesus sent out his disciples to carry on his mission, so we need to be ready to call others into the mission. Let's invite them to step out and see God work through them.

CHAPTER 5

Characteristics of a Mature Missionary Disciple

The goal of this chapter is to further describe what a mature missionary disciple looks like, by outlining the main areas that comprise a disciple's formation and progress in stages of growth.

Bringing those we evangelize to mature discipleship is the thesis of this book. Drawing from the biblical testimony and the tradition of the Church, as well as from our experience in helping young people grow to Christian maturity, we have identified various elements in effective formation. Let's review the basics of our presentation thus far.

First of all, we must be clear about the goal. The ultimate goal is the life of heaven. The proximate goal is growing in the imitation of Christ. John Paul II identifies, as the fundamental objective of formation, "an ever-clearer discovery of one's vocation and the ever-greater willingness to live it so as to fulfil one's mission."[81]

"Vocation" is from the Latin term *vocare*, which means "to call." The goal of formation, then, is to become who we are *created* and *called* to be in Christ. This call is the "vocation to holiness, that is, the perfection of charity."[82]

Second, we have seen that growing in holiness is a *process*, a series of steps. The further a person is from the goal of mature Christian discipleship, the longer it usually takes to reach the goal. Progress from one stage to another requires *change*, mainly concerning belief and behavior.

This process has had certain common, essential elements over the centuries of Church history, but it has taken various forms. Because the culture is now largely post-Christian, it no longer supports growth to mature discipleship, and we can't assume that adults, even if sacramentally initiated, have experienced conversion. Our times require new methods and processes. A process that leads a person to Christian maturity is effective if it is built on initial steps that foster authentic, integral conversion.

In this process of helping people grow to maturity, we have identified key vehicles. The principal vehicle is a formation environment, or community, in which disciples learn to live in daily committed love of God and others. Within the formation community, various meetings provide opportunities for new disciples to live and learn about the Christian life and the faith. These include meetings for prayer and teaching, as well as men's and women's small group meetings, which offer friendship and opportunities for accountability, personal sharing, growth in wisdom, and training in a communal approach to life and faith. The formation program also provides a way for new disciples to serve the mission initiative and witness to their faith.

All of this requires a leadership structure. Leaders must be identified and trained. They must be able to provide guidance and counsel for individuals throughout the formation process.

We now turn our attention to a more detailed description of what mature discipleship looks like and key areas that the formation process must address in order for disciples to mature.

Foundational Principles

Before describing the characteristics of a mature disciple, we want to propose three foundational principles that inform our approach to communicating and teaching the content of formation: grace, free cooperation, and a proper understanding of the human person.

Grace

The first principle is the principle of grace. God takes the initiative in our lives. He is the One who calls us to live fully as the person he has created and redeemed us to be, in the image of the triune God. All this is manifest in the incarnate Son, who is both the source of our life and the model we imitate.

What is the ultimate goal of God's initiative in our life? "Divinization," or deification—a sharing in the supernatural life of God—which is only possible if God makes it possible.

Matthew records an episode in which the disciples recognize the all-encompassing truth of God's call. On hearing Jesus' difficult teaching on sexuality, divorce, and riches, the disciples "were greatly astounded and said, 'Then who can be saved?' But Jesus looked at them and said, 'For mortals it is impossible, but for God all things are possible'" (Matthew 19:25-26, NRSVCE). Because God takes the initiative, all things are possible.

Free Cooperation

Our second principle is that growth toward Christian maturity requires that the maturing disciple freely cooperate with God's grace. Disciples must *respond* to God's call. As St. Augustine said, "God created us without us: but he did not will to save us without us" (*Catechism,* 1847, citing St. Augustine's *Sermo* 69.11.13). And so we are to "work out [our] own salvation with fear and trembling" (Philippians 2:12).

To this end, we must cooperate *actively* with the Lord's grace; we don't sit around waiting for God to change us. This cooperation involves using our minds to learn what is true and exercising our wills to make good choices. How do we cooperate with grace? By deciding to put ourselves in environments and relationships that help us grow; by trying to put into practice the wisdom and approaches our leaders teach in the formation program; by learning about and growing in virtue; by seeking counsel; by striving to live a daily life of faith and repentance; by asking for prayer.

For their part, leaders must respect the free will of the disciple. God calls disciples, and we can trust that he will work within them, but ultimately, they are responsible for their choices. Leaders, although their role is secondary, can do much, within the second principle, to foster growth in disciples as they respond to God's grace. As St. Paul tells us, "I planted, Apollos watered, but God gave the growth" (1 Corinthians 3:6).

Our role as leaders is to create the environment and foster the relationships that facilitate and encourage an encounter with God. We must be prayerful and discerning in our discipling. We have learned, while counseling people in formation, that although we teach and offer wisdom, much of what we do is simply listen and ask questions that help them discern the word and will of the Lord for them.

In this sense, the formation process is personal. Certainly God's call has a universal dimension to it—that is, it has an objective nature that applies to every human person. Yet Pope John II reminds us that "the human being is always unique and unrepeatable, someone thought of and chosen from eternity, someone called and identified by his own name."[83] As such, there is a unique and particular call for each person; there is a particular way that self-giving love in the image of the Trinity is concretely expressed in each person's life. A "program" of formation with a curriculum is necessary, but the formation content has individual application.

And so we return to a point we have made repeatedly: maturing disciples need more than programs. In this regard, I (Gordy) sometimes think of one of my favorite movies, the classic 1989 film *Field of Dreams*. In the movie, a farmer in Iowa hears a mysterious voice one night, urging him to build a baseball diamond in one of his cornfields. "If you build it, he will come," the voice says. The townspeople think he has lost his mind, but the farmer, at considerable financial sacrifice, builds the ball field, and eventually, famous baseball players show up.

It worked in the movie, needless to say, but my point in mentioning this beloved film here is simply this: in order to establish an effective formation program, we must do more than simply "build it." The right leadership, processes, and structures won't automatically produce mature Christians.

A Proper Understanding of the Human Person

Our third principle is this: our approach to formation needs to be founded on a renewed *theological anthropology*. "Theological anthropology" is a technical term that refers to a proper understanding of the human person in the purpose and design of God. At the beginning of our formation courses, we often repeat a verse from St. Paul's Letter to the Romans: "Do not be conformed to this world but be transformed by the renewal of your mind, that you may prove what is the will of God, what is good and acceptable and perfect" (12:2).

Many of those we are forming have lived, and are living, "in the world," as understood in the New Testament sense of thinking, valuing, believing, and living in a way that is contrary to the Lord and his ways. In this sense, as Scripture says, Christians must "not love the world or the things in the world" (1 John 2:15). Often, because we live in the world, our way of thinking has been formed by the world.

A properly developed and articulated theological anthropology is particularly important today because we are experiencing "an eclipse of the truth about man."[84] Many have forgotten God, live as though he does not exist, and have removed him from their understanding of the identity of the human person. Because the world has rejected the truth that a human being is a person and not a thing, we now live in what Pope St. John Paul II described as a "culture of death."[85] Selfishness characterizes this worldview, leading to the disregard for and dispatching of human life when it no longer has utility; the reduction of sexuality to selfish pleasure; the advancement of the idea of subjective gender; and the oppression of peoples for power, greed, and other forms of personal gain.

Our formational teaching needs to be derived from and solidly founded upon a strong and positive view of the human person as a creature of inestimable dignity, created in the image of God and made for relationship with God. It is this view of the human person that made St. Catherine of Siena exclaim,

> What made you establish man in so great a dignity? Certainly the incalculable love by which you have looked on your creature in yourself! You are taken with love for her; for by love indeed you created her, by love you have given her a being capable of tasting your eternal Good. (*Catechism*, 356, citing *Dialogue* 4, 13, "On Divine Providence")

Human persons in the image of God were created or "willed" to be male and female (see *Catechism*, 369, citing Genesis 2:7, 22). Maleness and femaleness are not just surface features but are essential to the identity of the human person in the image of God. The relational and communal vocation of the human person, with the call to self-gift, originates from the purpose and design of God in creation.

The teaching of the *Catechism* on Man (355–384) is a seminal reference for the Christian view of the human person and should be required study for all leaders engaged in formational teaching. It is essential that our formation content and the formation communities we establish be deeply informed by this profound theological anthropology.

Characteristics of a Mature Missionary Disciple

If our task is to form mature missionary disciples, we should have some idea of what a missionary disciple looks like. The grace of God, of course, works wonderfully to bring about in each person a unique set of traits. Still, we can gain an idea of the "portrait" of a disciple by asking: "What are the central characteristics of a missionary disciple of Christ? What are the fundamental habits and practices that mark a follower of Jesus?"

We have attempted to capture some of the main characteristics under the seven headings that follow.

1. Communion with God

A mature Christian disciple pursues a deep, abiding communion with God, reflected in faithful patterns of personal and corporate worship and prayer.

> The desire for God is written in the human heart, because man is created by God and for God; and God never ceases to draw man to himself. Only in God will he find the truth and happiness he never stops searching for: "The dignity of man rests above all on the fact that he is called to communion with God." (*Catechism*, 27, citing Vatican Council II, *Gaudium et Spes* 19,1)

We have established repeatedly the fact that a relationship with God is the source, center, and ultimate goal of the life of a disciple. The call to discipleship begins with an invitation from the Lord to enter into a personal relationship with him.

The first disciples were drawn to Jesus because they discovered in him the fulfillment of all they longed for in human life, so much so that they left all to follow him. From that moment on, their lives revolved around Jesus—being with Jesus, sharing life with him, listening to his words. This is true not only for those who followed Jesus as his disciples during his earthly ministry but for all disciples at all times. A disciple daily lives and shares life with Jesus. Conversion is the beginning of a lifelong journey of continually growing closer to the Lord, until we know that complete and perfect communion with him in the life to come.

Disciples experience and express their relationship with the Lord primarily through a life of prayer. Pope St. John Paul II wrote,

> Prayer develops that conversation with Christ which makes us his intimate friends: "Abide in me and I in you" (Jn 15:4). This reciprocity is the very substance and soul of the Christian life, and the condition of all true pastoral life.[86]

Prayer is foundational in the Christian life. Without prayer it is impossible to make any progress in the Christian life, much less grow to be a mature disciple. Thus, helping people learn about prayer and about how to grow in prayer is an early and ongoing priority in discipleship formation.

Our Catholic spiritual tradition is a rich and diverse source regarding the practice of prayer. "Many and varied *spiritualities* have been developed throughout the history of the churches" (*Catechism*, 2684, emphasis in original), flowing in large part from the Church's many religious orders and movements, each of which has developed a distinctive spirituality. Although an outline for how to practice personal prayer is outside the scope of this book, we can offer elements that are central to a life of prayer as well as things we have learned as we help young disciples learn to pray.

In one of the shortest verses in the Bible, St. Paul exhorts believers to "pray without ceasing" (1 Thessalonians 5:17, NRSVCE). How often should a Christian pray? Well, according to St. Paul, all the time, without ceasing, constantly.

Clearly Paul is not suggesting that we pray all the time in a formal sense and do nothing else. Rather, "praying without ceasing" means living our life in such a way that we are continually aware of God's presence. As the *Catechism* says, "'We must remember God more often than we draw breath.' But we cannot pray 'at all times' if we do not pray at specific times, consciously willing it" (2697, citing St. Gregory of Nazianzus).

Establishing habits and practices of prayer and other spiritual disciplines is key to cultivating awareness of God's presence. These practices are both personal and corporate. Personal practices are those we do on our own, and corporate practices are those we do with our housemates and the communities of faith to which we belong. Both types are essential.

It's important to emphasize good foundations as we help people develop their prayer life, not overwhelming them with too many options and resources. One of the first practices a young disciple must learn is the habit of daily personal prayer. On a practical level, it helps to establish a regular time, preferably at the beginning of the day, in a set location and following a certain pattern.

The length of time for prayer depends on a person's life circumstances and spiritual maturity. A college student may have lots of time to pray but may not be spiritually advanced enough to pray for long periods. We want people to experience success in developing the daily habit of prayer, so setting an achievable goal is important. Fifteen minutes is good for a beginner, increasing gradually to thirty minutes and perhaps, during certain seasons of life, to one hour.

A daily personal prayer time will look different from one person to the next and from one season of life to another, but certain elements should always be present. Prayer is relational, as we must continually remind those we are forming in prayer. To this end, the *Catechism* teaches, there are forms of prayer that are fitting to the way a human being relates to God. These are "praise and thanksgiving, intercession and petition (2098).

We praise God for his greatness, for who he is, in and of himself. We thank God for his goodness toward us, acknowledging that everything is a gift from him. In intercession we pray for the needs of others. To intercede is to be united with those for whom we pray; we accept the invitation from the Lord to participate with him in bringing his grace to others. In petition we ask the Lord for the things we need: "Give us this day our daily bread," the Our Father says.

We know that we are rightly relating to God when our prayer includes praise, thanksgiving, intercession, and petition. In addition, repentance and asking forgiveness should be part of our daily prayer. As the Our Father makes clear, we not only petition God for our needs but ask him to "forgive us our trespasses."

As prayer is relational, it is also conversational. We not only speak to God but also listen to him as he speaks to us. Listening to God in prayer often takes the form of meditation, whereby we spend time in silence, slowly reading and rereading something from Scripture or another spiritual source, paying attention to what moves us in the reading. *Lectio divina*, an ancient form of meditation, is an excellent way for a young disciple to learn to listen to the Lord in prayer, choosing Scripture from the daily Mass readings, the Liturgy of the

Hours, the Bible, or other spiritual books. It can help to keep a journal, recording thoughts, inspirations, and the things we hear the Lord saying to us in prayer.[87]

Growing in prayer involves a spiritual battle, a fact of which we might need to remind those who are new to prayer, so they do not become discouraged:

> [P]rayer is a battle. Against whom? Against ourselves and against the wiles of the tempter who does all he can to turn man away from prayer, away from union with God. . . . The "spiritual battle" of the Christian's new life is inseparable from the battle of prayer. (*Catechism*, 2725)

Because prayer is essential to the Christian life—and because it requires real effort and struggle—it is important that we provide regular opportunities for those growing to Christian maturity to talk about their prayer life during one-on-one meetings and small group meetings. In those settings, we can provide counsel and encouragement to help others advance in prayer. Within the formation process, we should also teach about and encourage personal disciplines such as regular Scripture reading and study, spiritual reading, frequenting the sacraments, fasting, and almsgiving.

It is not enough to pray on our own, however. The relationship that God invites us into is both personal and communal. Therefore habits of prayer in the life of the disciple must include the communal. We see this in the earliest days of the Church following the outpouring of the Holy Spirit on the day of Pentecost:

All who believed were *together*. . . . And day by day, attending the temple together and breaking bread in their homes, they partook of food with glad and generous hearts, praising God and having favor with all the people. (Acts 2:44, 46-47, emphasis added)

Liturgical prayer is the communal prayer of the Church. This is public prayer, the worship of the Church as a whole, and it has certain established rhythms.

The Tradition of the Church proposes to the faithful certain rhythms of praying intended to nourish continual prayer. Some are daily, such as morning and evening prayer, grace before and after meals, the Liturgy of the Hours. Sundays, centered on the Eucharist, are kept holy primarily by prayer. The cycle of the liturgical year and its great feasts are also basic rhythms of the Christian's life of prayer. (*Catechism*, 2698)

We give special attention in our formation process to honoring the Lord's Day. In the past, it was a nearly universal practice for Christians to approach Sunday as a day of rest from work. Today, however, though most serious Catholics remain faithful to the obligation to attend Sunday Mass, few set aside the day as a whole in order to "cultivate their familial, cultural, social, and religious lives" (*Catechism*, 2184, citing *Gaudium et Spes*, 67, 3).

In our formation communities, we begin the Lord's Day on Saturday evening with special prayers and a meal, followed by opportunities for rest and recreation together as brothers and sisters in Christ. Helping young disciples appreciate the full meaning of the Lord's Day and find practical ways to honor it is a powerful antidote to a secular, consumerist, and entertainment-saturated culture that makes it difficult to lift one's eyes to the eternal things that are above (see Colossians 3:1-3).

2. Communion with Others

Mature Christian disciples live their life in deep relationships of communion and friendship with other brothers and sisters in committed Christian love.

Some of the women who are leaders in our formation work developed a Scripture-related resource entitled *Made for Relationship*. This phrase captures the essence of the discipleship call.

In the previous section, we identified relationship or communion with God through a life of personal prayer as essential and foundational. But just as the disciples of Jesus share life with him every day, so also they share life with one another.

In the Scriptures, the command to love God is always followed by the command to love one's neighbor (see Matthew 22:34-40; Mark 12:28-34). Love of God and love of neighbor are inseparable. Created in the image of God, we are called to manifest the image of God in our communion with other persons.[88]

Living with others is part of the good of being human, of being part of the human race. God dwells in his people:

"I will live in them and walk among them,
and I will be their God,
and they shall be my people." (2 Corinthians 6:16)

God has "willed to make men holy and save them, not as individuals without any bond or link between them, but rather to make them into a people who might acknowledge him and serve him in holiness" (*Catechism*, 781, citing *Lumen Gentium*, 9).

Most people who are serious about growing in the Christian life understand the importance of having supportive relationships with other believers in order to grow in their relationship with the Lord. However, if we think about our relationships with other Christians primarily as a *means* to help us grow in the Lord, we miss the full significance of the Lord's call to join our lives with others. St. Paul uses the image of the body to convey the essential and vital nature of our relationship with other Christians:

> For just as the body is one and has many members, and all the members of the body, though many, are one body, so it is with Christ. For by one Spirit we were all baptized into one body—Jews or Greeks, slaves or free—and all were made to drink of one Spirit. (1 Corinthians 12:12-13)

We are united spiritually with all the members of Christ's body. God has so designed the body of Christ that we need one another in order to be complete.

Our unity with other believers is universal in nature, but it's primarily lived out in a particular way, in a particular place, with particular people. Much of the New Testament teaching on the life of the early Christian community emphasizes this "particular" notion of Church. It's clear from biblical testimony that the Christian life is meant to be lived in relationships of love, commitment, and mutual obligation.

When the New Testament speaks of the shared life to which Christians are called, it uses *family* as a primary image. We tend to think about Church mainly as a structure or set of programs. A family is a different reality. Let's revisit the family model here in terms of what a mature disciple looks like.

A family is, first, a type of relationship. It is a group of human beings who have a common origin, a common identity, and a way of life together. Our family relationships extend to everything in our lives. When we are in need, we usually turn first to our family members. We even expect that, because we are of the same family, we ought to help each other. There's a certain stability and permanence to family relationships as well.

I (Gordy) recall a conversation some years ago with one of my teenage children. "Dad," he remarked, "I don't think you're the kind of person with whom I would want to have a relationship." I replied, "Well, Son, we really don't have any choice about that. We have a relationship. I'm your father, and you're my child. That will never change. All we can choose is whether we will have a good relationship or a bad relationship."

Relationships today are increasingly compartmentalized, fragmented, and limited—even within the Church. Fostering stable, committed, family-like relationships among believers should be a priority for local church life. We make this a pastoral priority in our formation work, so that young disciples understand the critical need to live community life well. The community is where Christian life is formed and lived, and in this it reflects the family, which is both the domestic church and a school of love.

> The home is the first school of Christian life. . . . Here one learns endurance and the joy of work, fraternal love, generous—even repeated—forgiveness, and above all divine worship in prayer and the offering of one's life. (*Catechism*, 1657)

Needless to say, we face real challenges today in helping young disciples enter into deep relationships of communion and friendship in the body of Christ. We are in relationship with one another because of the life that we share in Christ, and we must teach and model a new orientation to relationships based on the biblical ideal. Often, however, people enter into relationships because of a common interest or task or attraction.

It's natural to be drawn to people who are like us. This isn't bad, but it limits us. The Lord calls us to be in relationship with many people we wouldn't choose as friends. Growing into Christian maturity involves learning to love all, and especially those we find difficult to love.

Christian relationships are based on *agape*—"selfless, sacrificial, and service-oriented love," in which we "build one another up" in Christ (1 Thessalonians 5:11). Many young people, however, have experienced unhealthy, unstable relationships that lead to loneliness, insecurity, feelings of isolation, and a constant need for approval. As a result, they tend to either avoid depth in relationships out of fear or approach relationships primarily out of need.

We've already considered the importance of commitment in Christian relationships, something largely absent in our culture. I (Gordy) recently noted this while watching a late-night talk show. An actor said that his latest relationship was going fine until his girlfriend started wondering about commitment.

"Why does she have to go mess up a good relationship by talking about commitment?" He then went on to say that it's absurd for anyone to stay in a relationship when things get tough. "Why torture yourself with drawn-out, painful discussions? Just drop it and move on." This typifies the modern approach to relationships.

In our culture, we measure the depth of a relationship by the strength of our emotions—how we feel. If the feelings fall away, we move on. In Christian relationships, however, we choose to do the right and loving thing regardless of how we feel. Action, not feeling, is the test of love.

To sum up, there is real work to be done in our formation processes and programs to help disciples reorient their relationships in Christ. When they experience stable, loving, committed relationships in Christ, they experience life the way God intended. There is healing, emotional health, joy, encouragement, accountability, and help in time of need. "Behold how good and pleasant it is" when brothers and sisters dwell together in unity, "for there the LORD has commanded the blessing" (Psalm 133:1, 3).

3. Growth in Understanding of Christian Truth

A mature Christian disciple continues to grow in understanding foundational Christian truth and experiences ongoing conversion to that truth.

I (Gordy) came of age in the 1970s, in the aftermath of the so-called sexual revolution. This was a time of significant change, particularly in the ways the culture at large viewed sexual norms and behavior. By the time I arrived at the Catholic high school I attended, it was more common than not among my classmates to accept the lie that sexual relations outside of marriage were morally permissible. I came to adopt this mindset.

Eventually I began to understand God's design in creating us in his image, the purpose of sexuality ordered to marriage and family in that design, and the higher meaning of love. My thinking about sexuality, formed by the world, needed to be transformed (see Romans 12:2).

Jesus tells the parable of two sons. One said he would not work in the vineyard and then did. The other said he would and then didn't (see Matthew 21:28-32). It's true that the measure of Christian love is revealed in our actions, but what goes on in our minds is also important.

The parable records that the son who ended up working in the vineyard had changed his mind (see Matthew 21:29). Perhaps when he changed his mind, he also began to change his thinking, actions, and habits. As Ralph Waldo Emerson wrote, "Sow a thought and you reap an action; sow an act and you reap a habit; sow a habit and you reap a character; sow a character, and you reap a destiny!"[89]

Some young disciples get impatient with the process of learning to think in a new way as Christians. They want to skip past the "why" and get to the "what." "Just tell me what to do and how to behave," they say. But Christian love originates in the heart. "Now that you have purified your souls by your obedience to the truth so that you have genuine mutual love, *love one another deeply from the heart*" (1 Peter 1:22, NRSVCE; emphasis added).

As previously noted, we tend to think that loving one another from the heart means loving with our affections or emotions. But in the Scriptures, the word "heart" refers to the *whole* of the innermost part of our being, not merely the emotions. It includes our soul, mind, and will, as well as our passions and appetites. Loving from the heart means loving with a purified soul, which begins with knowing and obeying the truth.

So what exactly is the problem with our minds? Why do our minds need to be transformed if we are going to be mature disciples?

We might be tempted to think that the main problem with our minds is that they are limited by our finite human nature. If we just knew more, we could solve all our problems. The solution, then, is simply to gain knowledge. Scripture, however, identifies another source of the problem. The problem with the mind is a spiritual one, and the transformation of the mind requires a spiritual solution.

One of the early lessons a young disciple must learn is that Christian life and growth involve warfare, as we briefly considered while discussing personal prayer. This is not a struggle against "flesh and blood" (Ephesians 6:12) but *spiritual* warfare. To grow and become mature, a disciple must recognize and engage in the spiritual battle every day.

The New Testament identifies three primary enemies in this conflict: the world, the flesh, and the devil. Traditionally these are called the three enemies of the soul.

> And you were dead in the trespasses and sins in which you once walked, following the course of this world, following the prince of the power of the air, the spirit that is now at work in the sons of disobedience—among whom we all once lived in the passions of our flesh, carrying out the desires of the body and the mind, and were by nature children of wrath, like the rest of mankind. (Ephesians 2:1-3, ESV)

The problem with our minds is that they are darkened and wounded because of sin (see Ephesians 4:17-18; Romans 1:28). Growth in Christ involves battling that darkness so that our minds are healed and transformed.

Why must we be particularly diligent today about the formation of the mind in the discipleship process? First, formation in understanding the mysteries and ways of God is generally not occurring as it once did in the family and Catholic education. Second, we live in an age of radical relativism that rejects the very idea of God—and even truth—and deconstructs an understanding of human nature created in the image of God. This is the air that people breathe today.

It is noteworthy that in the early Church, pre-baptismal instruction primarily focused on moral formation, and post-baptismal catechesis emphasized the mysteries of the faith. The latter was called the *mystagogy*. In evangelization and formation today, we call adults to complete their Christian initiation through acts of faith, repentance, and conversion and to change the way they live. We need to restore some form of the mystagogy. This is what we are trying to do in our formation process with young adults, to lead them ever deeper into the truths of the faith.

It is important to strike the right balance in our instruction between practical, lived Christianity and the explanation of Christian truth. Approaches to formation can err in either direction. There are some excellent catechetical initiatives and institutes that have emerged in our day, but we must not think that someone is a mature disciple simply because they have completed a catechetical program and can articulate the faith. I have met many young disciples who have some level of theological training but struggle in their spiritual and moral lives. Yet growing in understanding the mysteries of our faith should help us live that faith more deeply.

Likewise, an approach to formation that is mainly behavioral and practical is deficient. Disciples today need to be convinced, on some level, regarding why they should believe and why they should live as the Lord asks. When they are convinced, they are also better equipped to answer when challenged.

As we help young people embrace the Christian life, we should also emphasize the need to develop humility and faith in relation to the truth. When I (Gordy) began my theological studies, one of my professors in particular impressed upon me the importance of approaching the mysteries of the faith with humility. He spoke of Moses' encounter with the burning bush as a paradigm in this regard (see Exodus 3:1-6). Moses knew he was in the presence of mystery and hid his face. Just so, the mysteries of our faith are holy things because they are the truths about God and his ways. We need humility because we do not see clearly and because the things of God are mysteries that we can never fully apprehend.

An attitude of humility also helps counter the view that "what's true for you may not be true for me, so let's agree to disagree." When it comes to the definitive and authoritative teaching of the Church, we help young disciples understand that this approach is not okay. Mature disciples, in humility, first question their own understanding rather than questioning the proposed truth with which they struggle.

To help our young disciples better understand the faith, our presentations differentiate between what is authoritative and what is not. In the process, we respect the principle of the "'hierarchy' of truths."[90] This doesn't mean that some truths are truer than other truths. Rather, the "hierarchy of truths" refers to a certain order or organic structure to the truths of the faith. Some are central and foundational, and others are understood in relation to those. The Trinity is the central mystery of faith (see *Catechism*, 234).

The Creed is a summary of the central mysteries, which include creation, original sin, redemption, incarnation, the paschal mystery, the mission of the Son and the Spirit, the second coming of Christ, and the Church. Reading and studying the *Catechism* and other works that elucidate the faith are necessary habits of the mature disciple.

A mature disciple approaches Christian truth with faith along with humility. Our minds will not be transformed simply through studying a truth of the faith. Our minds are transformed as we encounter—with the help of the Holy Spirit—the truths and mystery of revelation, cooperate with grace, and yield to that Spirit who enlightens and transforms our thinking.

4. Delight in the Law of the Lord (Psalm 1:2)

A mature Christian disciple lives Christ's teaching on the moral law in daily life and personal relationships.

Some years ago, I (Gordy) developed and taught a course on basic Christian morality for university students in our formation program. I opened the class with a pop quiz asking the students to list, in order and from memory, the Ten Commandments. Most were able to name some, but only a few could identify all ten.

Ignorance of the commandments is only part of the challenge today. Loving the law of the Lord and delighting in his commands, as Scripture exhorts us to do, is foreign to the contemporary worldview, which perceives law as contrary to freedom. But freedom is not the opportunity to do whatever we want. It's the ability to act in a truly human way—that is, according to the image of God, in whom we are created. Knowing and living the commandments is essential to following Jesus in an immediate and practical sense.

Rather than moralizing—turning the Christian life into rules kept by human willpower—our goal is to help disciples who have encountered Christ in the power of the Spirit to see the new way of life that Christ has for them. As with all things in the Christian life, we understand the commandments in relationship to humanity's fundamental vocation—that is, the call to communion with God and one another. God gave the commandments to the Israelites in the context of establishing the covenant and forming a people (see Exodus 20:2-17; Deuteronomy 5:7-21). Jesus ultimately summarizes them under the heading of the two great commandments:

> You shall love the Lord your God with all your heart and with all your soul and with all your mind. This is the great and first commandment. And a second is like it: You shall love your neighbor as yourself. On these two commandments depend all the Law and the Prophets. (Matthew 22:37-40, ESV)

The commandment of love is the lens through which we understand the Ten Commandments. In short, if you want to know what love looks like, look at the commandments. They're not arbitrary rules imposed by God; rather, they have their origin in the character of God, who is love.

We see again the importance of the anthropological principle. The moral law corresponds with human nature as created by God. The *Catechism* teaches that God who created man out of love also calls him to love" and that this is "the fundamental and innate vocation of every human being. For man is created in the image and likeness of God who is himself love" (*Catechism*, 1604).

Thus the actions prohibited by the commandments correspond to the intrinsic good of God and others. In this sense, the law belongs to the natural order, the so-called natural law. In keeping the commandments, not only do we act in a way that honors the dignity of others created in the image of God, but we also act in accord with our own dignity.

There can be a temptation to adopt a minimalist approach to the commandments. To avoid this, we must ask ourselves what God intended when he gave us the commandments. What is the positive and fundamental human good that the commandments aim to preserve?

We can see this approach reflected in Pope St. John Paul II's discussion of the commandment "You shall not kill":

> As explicitly formulated, the precept "You shall not kill" is strongly negative: it indicates the extreme limit which can never be exceeded. Implicitly, however, it encourages a positive attitude of absolute respect for life; it leads to the promotion of life and to progress along the way of a love which gives, receives and serves.[91]

"Do not kill" is a command to recognize the dignity of human life, to respect life, and to preserve life. The commandment essentially is a command to love.

Jesus' teaching on the moral law takes this a step further in the Sermon on the Mount. Along with the commandments, understood in their fullest sense as categories of moral action ordered to love, Jesus proposes the Beatitudes as an ideal for our moral life. The Beatitudes, the *Catechism* says, "reveal the goal of human existence, the ultimate end of human acts: God calls us to his own beatitude" (1719). The Beatitudes manifest the true ideal and the end to which the commandments aim.

A mature disciple learns that following the moral law in the context of the great commandments of love and the Beatitudes is the way of true freedom. Blessed are those whose

delight is in the law of the LORD,
and on his law they meditate day and night. (Psalm 1:2, NRSVCE)

We are blessed because we live according to God's design for us, by God's power, and as he intended.

When we teach about the moral law and propose the high ideal of Christ's way of life, this brings up the problem of sin. "I do not understand my own actions," Paul exclaims. "For I do not do what I want, but I do the very thing I hate" (Romans 7:15). The temptation for a young disciple, when confronted with failures in obeying the moral law, is either to give way to self-condemnation or to abandon the ideal. "God knows my weakness and really doesn't expect me to strive to become *perfect*."

This is the problem of the rich young man in Mark's Gospel (see 10:17-22). Jesus identifies the commandments as the way to life, but the young man says he has followed them since childhood. Jesus then reveals the true meaning of the commandments when he tells the man to sell everything, give to the poor, and come follow him. The young man walks away sad. He is more attached to his many possessions than to the Lord.

The disciples meanwhile are confounded by this high ideal.

> They were exceedingly astonished and said among themselves, "Then who can be saved?" Jesus looked at them and said, "For human beings it is impossible, but not for God. All things are possible for God." (Mark 10:26-27, NABRE)

The *Catechism* states, "The Law of the Gospel 'fulfills,' refines, surpasses, and leads the Old Law to its perfection" (1967; citing Matthew 5:17-19). The law of the Gospel is the law of grace. In the new covenant, we are justified by the saving work of Jesus Christ, not because we follow the law.

This doesn't mean that we are free from following the moral law, for it remains the will of God for the Christian life. Through faith and the sacraments, the Holy Spirit dwells in us and gives us the disposition and ability to act in charity. Frequent participation in the Sacraments of Penance and the Eucharist, as well as turning to the Lord daily in repentance and receiving his mercy—these are the primary means of grace that help the Christian disciple make progress in living the moral life and coming to delight in the law of the Lord.

5. Growth in Virtue

A mature Christian disciple pursues growth and seeks mastery in Christlike character and virtue.

Knowing the moral law and deciding to live morally is one thing; actually living the way we have decided to live in Christ is another. To become "perfect, as your heavenly Father is perfect" (Matthew 5:48) requires that we actively grow in virtue. As the Letter of James reminds us, "Be doers of the word, and not merely hearers who deceive themselves" (1:22, NRSVCE). Until a person learns to act in a determined and consistent way in accordance with the good and the true, progress in the Christian life will be slow. Moreover, without growth in virtue, many people revert to old habits of sin and even abandon the faith.

The classical definition of virtue is a "habitual and firm disposition to do the good" (*Catechism*, 1803). Further, the *Catechism* says that virtue

> allows the person not only to perform good acts, but to give the best of himself. The virtuous person tends toward the good with all his sensory and spiritual powers; he pursues the good and chooses it in concrete actions.
>
> The goal of a virtuous life is to become like God. (1803, citing St. Gregory of Nyssa)

If we're only disposed to act in a good way sporadically, we aren't virtuous. When our actions and thoughts are consistently oriented to the good, then we are living virtuously.

The more virtuous we become, the more we reflect the goodness of God, in whose image we are created. Jesus, fully God and fully man, is the model of virtue. Our aim in the Christian life is to become like Christ (see Romans 8:29).

In order to be formed in the virtues, we must know what the primary virtues are in the Christian life. There are two groups of foundational virtues: (1) the cardinal virtues of prudence (practical wisdom), fortitude (courage), temperance (self-control), and justice; and (2) the theological virtues of faith, hope, and love.

The cardinal virtues are natural human virtues: they belong properly to human nature. We can know them by reason and acquire them by our own effort. "They make possible ease, self-mastery, and joy in leading a morally good life" (*Catechism*, 1804). The cardinal virtues perfect our intellect, enabling us to know the true good; strengthen our will so that we choose in accordance with the good; and govern our passions (emotions) so that they are ordered to the good.[92]

We teach about all the cardinal virtues in our formation work, but we pay particular attention to fortitude and temperance. These can be the most difficult for young people, and they're critical. Young disciples can easily give up, become impatient, fail to press through difficulty, succumb to fear, and be inconsistent in their obligations, resolutions, and commitments. Growth in the cardinal virtues enables them to move from service of self to love and service of others.

Certain aspects of the formation process can help young disciples grow in virtue. Role models are crucial: older and wiser brothers and sisters in the Lord who can teach, model the Christian life, offer wisdom and accountability, and encourage growth in virtue. Formation communities are equally important, offering committed relationships and consistent ways of sharing life and being on mission, as we have seen. One of the most effective ways to cultivate virtue is to live with others in an intentional way: sharing meals, praying together, doing chores, and keeping one's things in order.

We encourage fasting and other ascetical practices to help train the body. These practices have fallen out of favor, but they are essential for the long and exacting work involved in gaining self-mastery in the power of the Spirit (see *Catechism*, 2342).

The theological virtues—faith, hope, and love—are supernatural virtues.[93] While the natural virtues make it possible to live natural human life well, we know that God invites us to share in his divine life. The theological virtues are given to us to make it possible to "participate" in God's life. We know them by faith, rather than reason, and they're "infused by God into the souls of the faithful" (*Catechism*, 1813). We don't acquire them through our own effort; we receive these gifts from God through the Holy Spirit.

The theological virtues enable us to love God. They also fortify our human virtues, directing them to the love of God. Even though human virtues can be acquired by our effort, it's difficult to make progress without divine help. As such, "[t]he theological virtues are the foundation of Christian moral activity; they animate it and give it its special character" (*Catechism*, 1813).

Christian growth—growth as a disciple of Christ—is not an exercise in willpower. First and always, it's a matter of grace. We need to teach young disciples to exert real effort in resisting evil and doing good, but we need to encourage them most of all to yield to the Holy Spirit and ask the Lord for his help.

6. Seeking God's Will

A mature Christian disciple prayerfully discerns and embraces God's call in vocation, mission, and occupation.

"For I know the plans I have for you, says the LORD, plans for welfare and not for evil, to give you a future and a hope" (Jeremiah 29:11).

There are different roads to conversion, and Our Lord draws each of us to himself along paths tailored to our needs. One of the roads for me (Gordy) was the longing for purpose and meaning in life. Early in my path toward conversion, I heard a basic talk about the gospel that featured four points: "God made me. God knows me. God loves me. God has a plan for me." These are elementary but life-changing points.

God has a plan for me, and that plan is rooted in who he created me to be and in his intimate knowledge of and love for me. Growing to maturity as a disciple involves embracing the truth that God has a plan or will for me, seeking that will, and embracing it when I discover it.

We have already identified vocation, in the broadest sense, as the call of the Lord for my life. The vocation of every

Christian is the universal call to holiness. Fundamentally, that call is the theme of this book. *We are called to be disciples.* Jesus says, "If any man would come after me, let him deny himself and take up his cross and follow me. For whoever would save his life will lose it, and whoever loses his life for my sake will find it" (Matthew 16:24-25). The call is total, encompassing our entire life.

In our formation work with young people, we often use the phrase "all of my life, for the rest of my life" to express this call. There are no degrees in the Christian call, as if some are called to a deeper or more radical commitment than the rest of us. The call to holiness, which is the perfection of charity, is universal.

The seemingly harsh words of Jesus found in Revelation—"because you are lukewarm, and neither cold nor hot, I will spew you out of my mouth" (3:16)—find their meaning in this context. Anything less than a total daily commitment to offer the whole of my being to love God and neighbor is a failure in discipleship and compromises my Christian witness. The prayer of St. Ignatius of Loyola beautifully expresses this total commitment:

> Take, Lord, and receive all my liberty, my memory, my understanding, my entire will—all that I have and call my own. You have given it all to me. To you, Lord, I return it. Everything is yours: do with it what you will. Give me only your love and your grace. That is enough for me.[94]

This surrendering of my life is the starting point for hearing and embracing God's will. Through discernment—the process of coming to know and understand God's call for my life—I arrive at my unique expression of the universal call to holiness. Though we are called to love everyone, we find ourselves in proximity to a relatively small set of "someones." It is here that God's plan for our life unfolds. We can't love all of humanity if we don't actually practice love with some particular humans. The choices we make give context and specificity to how we live out the call to discipleship.

Mature disciples understand that the Lord has a plan for them and approach choices in life prayerfully, thoughtfully, and deliberately. This is the foundation for hearing and saying yes to God's will, setting our direction in life. My decision to marry Teresa focuses how I live out the call to holiness. I don't need to discern whom I am called to love when I wake up tomorrow. She is there right next to me, and the Lord has blessed us with six children, their spouses, and grandchildren. These are the first "someones" for whom I daily lay down my life.

Some of the decisions we make in regard to the Lord's call are big, weighty, life-determining decisions. Most are small daily decisions. The weighty, life-direction-setting decisions—such as whether I am going to marry, be a priest, be a religious, or remain single—provide the context for my daily decisions as I strive to be faithful to my call. The quality of our response to the disciple's call is demonstrated by how we actually live, through the choices we make.

As we have seen, John Paul II identified adolescence and young adulthood as *"particularly significant and decisive moments* for discerning God's call and embracing the mission entrusted by Him."[95] The choices and commitments during this season of life—in terms of career choices, state in life, where to live, what Christian community to associate with, and so on—shape our future. A mature disciple brings these foundational decisions to the Lord in prayer and seeks wise counsel and guidance. Effective formation will help young persons identify the important decisions they need to make and guide them in making those decisions well.

Not everything in the Christian life needs to be discerned in this way. We already know a great deal about God's call for our lives. I don't need to discern whether or not I should pray, obey the moral law, study and meditate on the mysteries of faith, or grow in virtue. I know that God's will is for me to become a person who is virtuous, who is Christlike.

> "I delight to do your will, O my God" (Psalm 40:8, NRSVCE).

Deciding to live and grow as a Christian in these ways is, however, a prerequisite for discerning life's major decisions. If we are not praying, we cannot hear the Lord well. If we are not growing in virtue and learning to live selflessly, our vocational choices may flow from the wrong motives. If we lack courage, we may hear the Lord's call but not be able to respond to it.

Discerning and making good vocational choices as a disciple involves detachment. The Lord invites us to offer the whole of our lives, freely and unreservedly, to him. "Here I am. . . . I delight to do your will, O my God" (Psalm 40:7, 8, NRSVCE).

In our formation work, we call young disciples to that ideal. We seek to help them grow in self-knowledge. When they have a deep understanding of their histories and temperaments, their strengths and weaknesses, their attachments and motivations, they become freer to surrender their lives.

Broadly speaking, we can think about following God's will in regard to foundational vocational choices as before and after. *Before* one makes those life-direction choices, radical discipleship involves learning to offer all the possibilities of our future unreservedly to the Lord. *After* we have made our permanent vocational choices, we express radical discipleship by faithfully living those choices.

7. Fruitfulness in Mission

A mature Christian disciple is actively engaged in mission and service in the kingdom of God:

> The Gospel offers us the chance to live life on a higher plane, but with no less intensity: "Life grows by being given away, and it weakens in isolation and comfort. Indeed, those who enjoy life most are those who leave security on the shore and become excited by the mission of communicating life to others." When the Church summons Christians to take up the task of evangelization, she is simply pointing to the source of authentic personal fulfilment. For "here we discover a profound law of reality: that life is attained and matures in the measure that it is offered up in order to give life to others."[96]

To be a disciple is to be on mission. It's not as if some disciples have a special call to mission and others do not. When Jesus called his disciples, he called them into relationship with himself, he called them into relationship with one another, *and* he sent them on mission. Disciples are called *and* sent.

The call to mission is made explicit in the first encounter between Jesus and Peter: "Then Jesus said to Simon, 'Do not be afraid; from now on you will be catching people'" (Luke 5:10, NRSVCE). Later we see Jesus sending out the seventy disciples (see 10:1-12). And before Jesus ascends to the Father, he commissions his followers to "go therefore and make disciples of all nations" (Matthew 28:19).

Disciples are called and chosen to be fruitful. "You did not choose me," Jesus says to his disciples, "but I chose you. And I appointed you to go *and bear fruit*, fruit that will last" (John 15:16, NRSVCE; emphasis added).

Fruitfulness is one of the marks of a mature disciple. The process of discipleship formation is complete only when the one being evangelized becomes an evangelizer.

> The person who has been evangelized goes on to evangelize others. Here lies the test of truth, the touchstone of evangelization: it is unthinkable that a person should accept the Word and give himself to the kingdom without becoming a person who bears witness to it and proclaims it in his turn.[97]

Sharing with others and wanting them to come to know what we have experienced is the natural fruit of the encounter with Jesus Christ. "From this loving knowledge of Christ springs the desire to proclaim him, to 'evangelize,' and to lead others to the 'yes' of faith in Jesus Christ" (*Catechism*, 429). Being compelled by the love of God to evangelize (see 2 Corinthians 5:14) is one of the marks of a deep and authentic conversion.

If we are to help young disciples bear fruit that will last, we must help them recognize and overcome within themselves the pervasive consumerism that characterizes our world today. A consumeristic society measures value according to the accumulation of experiences and things. At its core are selfishness and radical individualism. Consumerism can even infect the way some Christians approach religion, seeing it as a commodity. Thus we have "cafeteria Catholics," who pick and choose teachings, practices, and even faith communities based on whether they suit them.

The call to discipleship is the antithesis of consumerism. Life is not about the accumulation of things: "For what will it profit a man if he gains the whole world and forfeits his soul? Or what shall a man give in return for his soul?" (Matthew 16:26, ESV). The question the disciple asks is not "What will I get?" but "What can I give?" "Whenever our interior life becomes caught up in its own interests and concerns," says Pope Francis, "there is no longer room for others, no place for the poor."[98]

Once again we see how crucial it is for our discipleship formation to be rooted in a proper theological anthropology. The human person is made not for self-concern but for self-gift. The call to give ourselves to God in worship, to live in selfless love in community, to offer our lives unreservedly to God in vocational choosing, and to submit our minds to an objective truth—these all involve confronting selfishness and accepting the invitation to embrace self-gift on the road to Christian maturity. To be sent in mission is yet another opportunity for disciples to give their lives away, to give all their lives for the rest of their lives.

The Lord calls every disciple to the primary mission of evangelization. The Church "exists in order to evangelize," and every member of the Church is called to participate in that mission.[99] Each disciple is personally called by name; every disciple must make a response. Every other expression of mission and service within the Church flows from and is informed by this evangelical imperative. What is the mission to which every Christian disciple is called? *Evangelization*!

As we noted earlier, the works of evangelization encompass many things. In the broadest sense, Jesus calls his disciples to the work of bringing the kingdom of God to the world. We are called to be salt, light, and leaven. Most Christians participate in the mission of the Church

> by engaging in temporal affairs and by ordering them according to the plan of God. . . . Therefore, since they are tightly bound up in all types of temporal affairs it is their special task to order and to throw light upon these affairs in such a way that they may come into being and then continually increase according to Christ to the praise of the Creator and the Redeemer.[100]

This extends to the full range of social, political, and economic realities. Included in that range, of course, are those closest to us, in our families and church communities. But it extends to all people we encounter, especially the neediest among us. Thus the mission can take many forms yet must never be detached from the essential proclamation: "*Humanity is loved by God! . . .* Each Christian's words and life must make this proclamation resound: God loves you, Christ came for you, Christ is for you 'the Way, the Truth and the Life!' (Jn 14:6)."[101]

Throughout this book, we have expressed the conviction that effective formation happens principally in the context of community. Faith is caught as well as taught. This is no less true for formation in mission. This means that our formation communities need to be "communities of missionary disciples."[102]

Our mission is a mission "*on behalf of* communion." Mission flows from communion and finds fulfillment in communion.[103] The community is a primary witness to the gospel (see 1 John 1:3). It follows that the disciple needs to be immersed in the life of the community, and the community needs to be a community on mission.

Sometimes our formation communities can be so immersed in fostering deep and life-giving relationships among their members that they become inward focused. People become so comfortable in their bubble that it is difficult for new people to break in. If our formation programs and communities are going to form an effective missionary spirit in disciples, they cannot be closed in on themselves. They must focus outward and have expressions of mission.

Pope Francis warns against "a Church which is unhealthy from being confined and from clinging to its own security."[104]

A community that loses its sense of commitment to mission loses its reason for being. "The intimate life of this community," wrote Pope Paul VI, "only acquires its full meaning when it becomes a witness, when it evokes admiration and conversion, and when it becomes the preaching and proclamation of the Good News."[105]

The community, then, ought to be a place where we strengthen, encourage, and support disciples who go out on mission. Even in the "going out," the communal dynamic is present. The lone evangelist is not the norm; Jesus sent his disciples out two by two.

As we said before, we should call young disciples to service and mission very early in the formation process. Often the best evangelizers are recent converts, because they are still close to the experience of conversion. I (Gordy) was evangelized by someone relatively new to the faith. I too was eager right away to share with others the newly rediscovered faith I was experiencing.

When we evangelize, our faith is strengthened, and our understanding grows. We have opportunities to explain the gospel and respond to questions and objections. These situations oblige new disciples to learn about and more deeply comprehend the faith. Even more, when new disciples experience the Lord working through them to the benefit of another or when they witness someone experiencing the presence and power of the Lord's mercy and grace, their own conversion is renewed and deepened.

CHAPTER 6

A Lifelong Vision for Adventurous Discipleship

The aim of this final chapter is to communicate a vision for lifelong discipleship. To become a disciple of Jesus Christ is to embark on a path marked by adventure, trial, fruit bearing, and suffering. The question we seek to answer in this chapter is, "How can we prepare people for the challenges they will face on the path of discipleship, and how can we encourage them to follow Christ with faith, hope, and love for the rest of their lives?"

L et's return to that short saying we frequently use to capture the heart of lifelong discipleship: "All of my life, for the rest of my life." Jesus has called us to offer *all* of ourselves (not just part) for the *rest* of our lives (not just for a season). Christ didn't call his followers only for a special intensive period of time. He didn't invite people to give a generous portion of time during their youth so that they could pursue their own goals and dreams thereafter. He called people for the duration of their lives.

We live in a world of constant flux. Attention spans have shrunk, and people want to keep their options open. Living a comfortable and pain-free life is a high priority for most of us. If things get hard or even unpleasant, we want to make a change and make it right away. Lifelong vocations—marriage and celibacy—which require us to persevere through periods of challenge, frequently suffer breakdowns in this climate.

In many respects, ours is not a heroic age. While we may need to make accommodations in the way that we make disciples in this social climate, it's important that we help people hear a countercultural call to radical discipleship. Once again, Jesus' practice of reaching out and calling people provides a pattern for us. There is a profound paradox in how he did this.

On the one hand, Jesus shocked the people of his day by reaching out to tax collectors, prostitutes, lepers, and even demoniacs. He offered a radical welcome to those who were on the margins—to the poor and downtrodden. He spoke to these people about the kingdom of God and encouraged them to trust in the provision of their Father in heaven. He healed multitudes, not because they were worthy, but because they were in need. Jesus was ready to unleash the power of the kingdom of God on their behalf. He offered a radical welcome to all.

On the other hand, Jesus shocked his contemporaries by placing the highest and most uncompromising demands on those who would be his disciples. Anyone who loved even father or mother more than Jesus was not worthy to be in his cohort (see Matthew 10:37). He told his followers that they had to lose their lives if they were to find and save their lives. He pointed them to the cross as the way to follow in imitation of him (see 16:24, for example).

Many people found Jesus' words too difficult, and they turned away. But Jesus didn't water down his demands. He continued to offer a radical call to discipleship. Was Jesus presenting an inconsistent message, offering a radical welcome along with radical demands?

Today we tend to set these two "radical" approaches in opposition to one another, and then we choose the one that we think most exemplifies the gospel. Some people conclude that if we are meant to give a radical welcome to everyone, then we cannot place any demands on them or call them to a transformed life; we just accept them as they are and leave it at that. Others are inclined to think that if we are to call people to radical discipleship, then we can't welcome all comers, most of whom are plainly unprepared for this calling.

But Jesus did both. He welcomed all who would listen, and he healed them unconditionally. He also demanded change— "Go, and do not sin again" (John 8:11). And at the right time, he called his followers to wholehearted discipleship.

In a cultural climate such as ours, with many people wounded and ill-equipped for a high call, we must offer an unconditional, radical welcome that invites people to encounter Jesus and find healing in him. But if we are to remain faithful to the gospel, we must also call people to receive the grace of God and be transformed in mind, heart, and practice. Admittedly, combining a radical welcome with a radical call to discipleship is not easy; we need to find ways to present both without compromising either. And the two are consistent with one another, for those who are forgiven much are often best equipped to love much and to respond with generous hearts (see Luke 7:47).

Witness, Narrative, and Story

Pope Paul VI captured something critical for understanding our present time: "Modern man listens more willingly to witnesses than to teachers, and if he does listen to teachers, it is because they are witnesses."[106] Pope Francis has said much the same thing: "Today too, people prefer to listen to witnesses."[107] What do they mean?

People today are ready to listen to those who live what they teach and who speak from their own experience. Human beings have always loved stories and narratives, but today the preference for learning by story is especially strong. Teaching remains essential, and we abandon it at our peril; but we will be much more effective communicators of the gospel if we provide ample testimony—concrete and authentic narratives of our experience—to surround and embody the teaching we give.

> Modern man listens more willingly to witnesses than to teachers, and if he does listen to teachers, it is because they are witnesses.

For many years in our student outreaches, we have offered seminars that provide an intensive presentation of the gospel to help people encounter Christ.[108] Time and again, students say that the plain, unadorned testimonies of their peers have the most impact on them—more than the well-prepared presentations given by our best speakers. Teaching and testimony go hand in hand, but it is frequently testimony that opens hearts and minds most effectively to the gospel. And when people are moved by the speakers, it is usually because these speakers also give *testimony* to how the teaching has impacted their lives.

To expand and broaden this point, let us consider our wider culture's fascination with stories and narratives. The media that dominates our popular culture—video (movies) and music—communicate narrative and story with great power. Young and old alike migrate toward their favorite movies or television series. Many popular songs, both secular and Christian, tell stories that pull at the heart and stir the emotions. We live in a world where, for better or worse, people reach for stories—powerful, violent, funny, or heart-rending. And these stories have an enormous ability to form minds and hearts.

As Christians, we are in possession of the greatest "story," or narrative, in the world. In fact, it is the one and true story of the world. The gospel of Jesus Christ is *the* great story, the adventure that all other adventures point to or derive from.

Too often we box our faith into a religious category. We think about our faith as defining our "religious identity" and quarantine it from the rest of life. But being a Christian—being a disciple of Jesus—is much more than a religious identity; it is much more than a set of beliefs, liturgical practices, or moral convictions (though these are essential). Becoming a

Christian means recognizing that Jesus Christ defines the story of the whole world.

When we become followers of Jesus, we are drawn into the true story that encompasses all other stories. There are no half measures here. The call to discipleship makes a claim on our whole lives, not just the "religious" part.

Consider the first followers of Jesus as we meet them in the pages of the Gospels—Peter, Andrew, James, and John. When they encountered Jesus, their lives were turned completely upside down. Becoming Jesus' disciple was not just a matter of taking on a new moral code or reading a certain holy book or attending a set of religious services. For these first disciples, it meant reshaping their whole lives around this person they had encountered. It meant becoming part of a new community of people. Nothing was the same.

> Becoming a Christian means recognizing that Jesus Christ defines the story of the whole world.

Here we need to be credible witnesses ourselves. All aspects of our lives—marriage, family, job, career, recreation, possessions, friendships—need to be configured around the person and teaching of Jesus. We don't have to do everything perfectly—no one does that. But if we seek to live this way—to configure all our "loves" around Christ—then our words will carry impact. We can't call people into a life of discipleship if we are not living this life ourselves.

When we call people to follow Jesus with their whole lives—with nothing held back—many respond with genuine faith, zeal, and joy. We see this happening powerfully among the generational cohort called millennials. Of course, it is not our words that persuade them: it is the power of Christ's own words and his call that reaches their hearts.

When people make a full response by offering their whole lives to Christ, a paradigm shift occurs. They move from thinking about Jesus and religion in terms of something *they* do, on their own terms, to seeing themselves caught up by Jesus into a great adventure not of their own making. The terms change. I am no longer crafting my own religious identity; I have been claimed and called by another. My will is still fully involved, but I am no longer in charge of the process. Now my task is to respond (or not) to the call of Jesus with all that this implies.

People have a desire, a hunger even, to be caught up in a truly meaningful narrative. They sense that their lives have meaning, and they grope to find what this purpose might be. If and when they sadly conclude that their lives have no clear meaning, they lose heart and meander into activities that distract them or that hide the apparent meaninglessness of their existence.

Why are modern audiences entranced by superhero movies? Why was a whole generation of young people mesmerized by Harry Potter and his momentous struggle against a dark and powerful foe?

In these stories there is abundant adventure and excitement, but even more, there is a purpose and a reason for struggling and fighting for what is right. Something big is at stake—usually the ongoing existence of the free world! How the characters respond makes a huge difference. All of us have a natural hunger to find a meaningful narrative that guides us through the challenges of life.

But a steady diet of superhero movies will not give purpose to our lives. Reading about Harry Potter defeating Lord Voldemort or about Frodo and Sam struggling to defeat Sauron cannot give meaning to our own existence. These adventures can stir our imagination and implant a desire for a noble life, but they can't give actual purpose to our lives.

Only the gospel of Jesus Christ—and this alone—offers a narrative that we can truly enter and there find meaning for our lives. When we recognize that we have been caught up in the great narrative of the gospel—that it has come knocking at our door—we grasp our faith in a new way. If we open the door, we can set out on a path of lifelong discipleship.[109]

Discipleship Crossroads

There is no precise map for the path of discipleship, no trail that is the same for all. Each of us will walk a unique road—led by the Spirit, led by the providential hand of our Father in heaven.

We know that discipleship is meant to be lifelong: we never stop growing as disciples, never stop walking on the track marked out for us. The apostle Paul speaks to this: "Not that I have already obtained this or have already reached the goal;

but I press on to make it my own, because Christ Jesus has made me his own" (Philippians 3:12, NRSVCE).

We too are called to "press on" to the end of our course. If there is no exact blueprint, there are typical stages in discipleship that we can identify. Knowing these can help us cooperate with the grace of Christ in being his disciples and in making disciples.

One of the primary aims of this book is to offer an outline of what formation in discipleship might look like. This occupied the previous five chapters. In this final chapter, we stand back and take a broader, panoramic view of the stages in discipleship. There are many ways to describe these stages. Here we identify three typical discipleship crossroads that—in one way or another—most followers of Christ will face during their lives.

When we are walking a path and come to a crossroads, we have a decision to make. Which way will I take from here? What is the best route to get me to my destination? Should I continue straight on or turn to the right or the left? Or should I turn back and return by the way I came?

We can't avoid discipleship crossroads. We have to face them and pray for the grace to continue on the path of costly discipleship.

The First Crossroads: Will I Cast My Lot with Jesus?

The first crossroads is also the true beginning of discipleship. Will I cast in my lot, throw down my nets, and set off down the track following Jesus? Or will I keep my options open, remain at a safe distance, or simply turn back and go home?

No one becomes a disciple without facing this crossroads at one time or another. No matter how long it takes or what steps brought us to this place, at some point we have to take the plunge and decide to follow. This decision *is* the act of faith; it is faith in action.

When Jesus called, Matthew left his tax booth (see Matthew 9:9). He acted on faith and began to follow Jesus. All of us who have faced this crossroads know that it is *grace* that carried us through and strengthened us to decide to follow. However much wrestling we may do, it is the grace of God, often operative through the prayers of others, that moves us to say yes to the Lord's invitation. But we have the ability to resist this grace and to decline the offer.

The classic case—which we have looked at before—that exemplifies this crossroads is that of the rich young man who approaches Jesus. He comes energetically and expresses a desire to follow God and to do his will. This man is already a "believer," not an atheist. He actually wants to serve God in some way.

But primarily, it seems, the young man wants to be justified in the life he is already living. He is hoping to be told, "You are doing just great. Keep it up, and you'll be fine."

And so Jesus reviews the basics: "Are you keeping the commandments of God?" "Yes," he says, "I have kept them from my youth." And now, feeling quite good about himself, the rich man asks the fateful question: "What do I still lack?" (Matthew 19:20). In Mark's version of the encounter, Jesus looks at him and *loves* him (see 10:21). Christ calls us because he *loves* us, not to make our lives miserable.

Jesus then gives this young man an enormous gift: the call to leave other things behind and to follow him personally. What is the response of this rich young man? He becomes sad because he has great possessions and cannot leave them behind. He isn't happy even with his many possessions; they cannot give him true joy. But at this point in his life, he can't leave them. And so he departs, a downhearted man.

In direct contrast, we have the story of Bartimaeus, a blind beggar, a man of no importance or standing. He places himself on the roadside as Jesus is passing by, and he cries out again and again for Jesus to have mercy on him. Others tell him to be silent, but he continues to call out.

Jesus hears and responds; he asks Bartimaeus what he wants. Bartimaeus asks to receive his sight, and Jesus immediately grants his request: his eyes are miraculously opened. And then, significantly, the Gospel says that Bartimaeus "followed him on the way" (Mark 10:52). The act of healing leads directly to the path of discipleship.

The rich young man, full of good deeds, could not find it in himself to follow Jesus; the cost was too high. The blind beggar, who received his sight as a sheer gift, gladly followed after him. Both found themselves at a crossroads: one turned back and went home, while the other cast in his lot and followed.

We can distinguish two distinct paths that approach this crossroads. The first path is that of the nonbeliever who is being drawn to consider Jesus and the claims that he makes. For the nonbeliever, Jesus really is a new figure, someone never before encountered or considered. There is a freshness and newness in this encounter but also great obstacles, because deciding to follow Jesus brings about a complete change of belief and life.

The second path is that of the baptized Christian who has been raised (more or less) in the faith and who has identified (more or less) as a believer throughout childhood and early adolescence. For this person, this first crossroads presents the question, "Will I really choose to be a follower of Jesus through my own faith and decision?"

The temptation for many young people raised as Catholics is to avoid this crossroads in the hope of maintaining some kind of religious affiliation with no real cost. We are all acquainted with the double-life syndrome: I claim to be a Christian, go to Mass or youth group on occasion, but during the rest of my life, I live (and want to live) the way everyone else does. Foolishly, people think they can have it both ways. They want to hold on to their lives on their own terms while at the same time make some gesture toward following Jesus. This never works. "No one can serve two masters" (Matthew 6:24).

We have encountered countless young people in their late teens and early twenties who face this crossroads. At present, the statistics aren't encouraging for this age cohort. Many young Christians and, sadly, especially many young Catholics, effectively abandon the practice of their faith in this transition period of early adulthood.

I (Dan) recall this crossroads in my life with great clarity. In high school, I wanted to keep some part of my faith intact, but I also really wanted to run my own life and not be bothered by the things of God. I avoided situations that might put me in the way of encountering God, because I didn't want to face this crossroads. My hope was that God would send his blessings from a distance and basically leave me alone.

In the end, I couldn't avoid facing this crossroads. With real struggle and through the prayers of many, I found my way across this intersection and onto the path of discipleship. It was only then that I really tasted the joy that comes on the far side of this crossroads, the joy of knowing Jesus and finding true freedom in him.

When we navigate this first crossroads and decide to cast our lot with Jesus, there is a flow of grace into our lives: joy, new power for living, and fresh zeal to make Jesus known to others. It is the joy and delight of the man who found the treasure hidden in the field and sold everything he had to buy the field and possess the treasure (see Matthew 13:44).

Once we are past this first crossroads, we may be tempted to think, "This is it. I have now made the key decision: I have become an intentional disciple of Jesus. I can now walk this path with ease and joy, serving the Lord to the end." But other crossroads lie ahead.

The Second Crossroads: Will I Turn Back in the Face of Hard Things?

For those who have navigated the first crossroads and have set out on the track of discipleship with determination, things get exciting. There is usually a sense of joy and new adventure—a lightness in our step. We experience God being close at hand, and we progress in the spiritual life rapidly, at least in certain areas. There is commonly a honeymoon period, when all seems good and relatively easy. The Christian life is great!

But this doesn't last (very) long. Soon we come up against more challenging issues that don't change easily. We might find ourselves out of our depth, engaged in mission or service that is daunting and difficult. We face new questions that are profoundly perplexing. Things begin to get hard. Why?

Some part of this is due to the things that oppose us—the world, the flesh, and the devil. We find opposition in the world around us; we experience the pull of our own desires, which lead us away from the things of God; and we discover that we have a personal enemy, the devil, who opposes us in many ways. Strikingly, it *seems* as if God is allowing these hard things and possibly even sending trials and difficulties our way.

Let's recall that just after Jesus was baptized by John, the Spirit led him out into the wilderness to be tested by the devil. We are called to face the same challenges that Jesus faced. Jesus will make use of these trials to sift our hearts and to purify them.

One of the clearest biblical examples of this kind of testing occurs in the Book of Exodus. The people of Israel were powerfully delivered from Egypt. They watched as the Lord conquered the Egyptians, who drowned in the Red Sea. But quite quickly the Lord led the Israelites into the desert, where they had no water and no food. They grumbled and asked Moses to lead them back to Egypt, to the land of their slavery, where at least they had food (see Exodus 15–16).

It didn't take long for the Israelites to give up and wish to turn back. But through Moses and his intercession for the people, the Lord provided water and food for them, and they continued on.

Another striking example of the second crossroads of discipleship appears in the Gospel of John, chapter 6, the Bread of Life Discourse. In the opening scene, Jesus quietly performs a great miracle, the feeding of the five thousand. This reveals him to be the Messiah who, like Moses, provides bread for the people to eat in the wilderness. In fact, the people are so stirred up that they want to take hold of Jesus and acclaim him as the king, the Messiah of Israel. But this is not the plan of the Father for Jesus.

Now comes the sifting of hearts. The next day, the crowds who were fed with the loaves realize that Jesus and the disciples have departed. The crowds follow them to the city of Capernaum. When they find Jesus, they ask him how he got there. Jesus doesn't answer their question directly. Instead, he cautions them against just seeking more "bread" to eat. He turns them away from the sign toward the reality, which is the true eternal food that the Son will give to them.

When asked about this bread, Jesus says solemnly that *he* is the true bread from heaven given by the Father. Some of the leaders take offense at this claim (no surprise), and they challenge him about what this means. Jesus is, after all, just a man from the town of Nazareth. Who is he claiming to be?

Jesus doesn't back down. In fact, he uses provocative language to challenge the people further. He says that his very flesh is food and his blood is drink. To have eternal life, one must eat his flesh and drink his blood.

As readers, we recognize that Jesus spoke here about the Eucharist and about the sacrifice for sins that he would offer on the cross. But the people listening were deeply scandalized. Here is John's report of what they said and did: "Many of his disciples, when they heard it, said, 'This is a hard saying; who can listen to it?'" (John 6:60). The result: "After this many of his disciples drew back and no longer went about with him" (6:66).

Notice that these are *disciples* who turn back and walk away. Jesus' hard words, in fact, were the occasion for many of his disciples to turn back; his words were difficult and challenging. These disciples came to this crossroads and decided not to continue.

> However it comes—and it may come more than once—we can be sure that we will find the cross in our path.

What does Jesus do? Does he chase after the disciples to call them back? Does he apologize for being too demanding? No, he turns and challenges even the twelve apostles: "Will you also go away?" (John 6:67). Jesus is testing them, leading them through a trial of their faith.

Peter, speaking for the Twelve, says, "Lord, to whom shall we go? You have the words of eternal life; and we have believed, and have come to know, that you are the Holy One of God" (John 6:68-69). The apostles pass the test; they successfully navigate this crossroads.

This second crossroads will look different for each of us. Often we don't even realize that we are being tested. Perhaps we are in the midst of a trial or a perplexing situation, and we are tempted to wonder if we should give up and go back to the life we had before. Sometimes this crossroads is a personal crisis in our lives. Sometimes it is a hard truth that we have difficulty accepting. Sometimes it comes because God asks us for something that we are not ready to give.

However it comes—and it may come more than once—we can be sure that we will find the *cross* in our path. This is truly a "cross road" that we must embrace. By embracing the cross and continuing on with Christ, we pass an important test, thus deepening God's action in us. Crucially, it was only after the disciples went through these kinds of tests that Jesus began to entrust himself to them and reveal to them more intimate and deeper truths.

During our years of student ministry, we have watched many young people reach this crossroads. Through prayer and the help of others, many, even most, have met the grace of God to continue on. But some do not, and this is always a source of grief and sadness.

We can see this diverse response in the parable of the sower. The same seed is sown, but it yields differing results, depending on how people respond to the word and the grace given (see Matthew 13:1-9, 18-23). A crucial part of becoming a *mature* disciple of Christ is facing and successfully navigating this second crossroads. Grace is always available if we are ready to receive it and act upon it.

The Third Crossroads: Reliance on God in the Midst of Apparent Defeat

This third crossroads might seem like just a version of the second, but we can distinguish it by when it occurs and what provokes it. The second crossroads often occurs early in the path of discipleship, in the first few years. The third crossroads typically happens later, and it often involves the temptation to discouragement and despair because of failure, real or apparent.

Consider the example of the apostle Paul. By the time he was writing the Second Letter to the Corinthians (between AD 55 and 57), he was a seasoned missionary and a leader in the early Christian movement. He had crisscrossed the Roman world and successfully founded many new local churches. Along the way he suffered a great deal (see the list of his hardships in 2 Corinthians 11:23-29); he was no stranger to severe physical hardship and personal rejection. He was well tested as a disciple.

Still, in the opening of his Second Letter to the Corinthians, Paul recounts his recent experience of mission in the province of Asia:

> For we do not want you to be unaware, brothers, of the affliction we experienced in Asia. For we were so utterly burdened beyond our strength that we despaired of life itself. Indeed, we felt that we had received the sentence of death. (2 Corinthians 1:8-9, ESV)

Paul was pushed to his limits and even beyond them; he "despaired of life itself" under the unbearable challenges that he faced. But when he came through this severe test, Paul was able to perceive its divine purpose: "But that was to make us rely not on ourselves but on God who raises the dead" (2 Corinthians 1:9, ESV). Paul, the seasoned apostle, still had something to learn about trusting in God. He was pressed, by the circumstances of his mission, to trust God even more deeply.

Hudson Taylor was a pioneering English Protestant missionary in the late nineteenth and early twentieth centuries. He founded an impressive mission society, the China Inland Mission. Through years of labor, in which he showed extraordinary trust in God, he saw many Chinese come to faith in Christ. The mission expanded, and many missionaries went inland to share the gospel with the Chinese.

But in the year 1900, the Boxer Rebellion erupted, a backlash against foreigners in China. Taylor's missionaries were in the crosshairs of the rebellion. Away on furlough, Hudson Taylor received the horrifying reports of the slaughter of his missionaries and their families. In the end, fifty-eight missionaries along with twenty-one of their children were killed in the rebellion. Taylor was so distraught by this news that he couldn't speak, he couldn't even pray—but he was somehow able to trust. His faith held firm in this awful test of his life's work.

Even in the case of a seasoned disciple, there can be much room to grow through hardship and testing. Many Christian leaders throughout the centuries have testified to the severe test of the third crossroads. The only way through it is by means of a deeper and more radical trust in God and his providence.

Some years ago, I (Dan) came across a newly published edition of the diaries of the Lewis and Clark Expedition (1804–06). With fascination I gobbled up the four hundred pages of daily diary entries that recounted the adventures of this thirty-person team as they traveled from St. Louis to the Pacific coast and back. What struck me most was how their experiences mirrored the life of a disciple.

At the beginning of their journey, Lewis and Clark traveled through relatively well-mapped lands and made significant progress. Though they were beginners and still learning the ropes, they made the greatest progress at the start. As they went along and gained experience, the way became paradoxically more difficult. The terrain became harder, the lands were not well mapped, and they finally had to abandon their boats and climb into the mountains. As they grew in skill and became more wilderness-wise, the way became steeper and harder.

> Christ our Lord brings us more fully into his own counsels and invites us to share more deeply in the cross—in his death and resurrection.

In the end, Lewis and Clark would have perished in the mountains except for the intervention of the native peoples, who provided them with horses and guided them across the mountains. With this help, they were able to complete the journey to the Pacific Ocean and make their way back again.

Isn't this a pattern for discipleship in Christ? We set out on the path with great energy and often make significant progress early on. But then we encounter hard things that slow us down and even tempt us to stop and go back. Finally we reach terrain that is steep and seemingly insurmountable. Almost despairing of life itself, we make it through by the grace of God and the help of others.

Paradoxically, as we grow in wisdom and virtue, the way seems to become harder and more challenging. Christ our Lord brings us more fully into his own counsels and invites us to share more deeply in the cross—in his death and resurrection. As we embrace this, we are changed into his image "from one degree of glory to another" (2 Corinthians 3:18).

There is no blueprint for how this will work out for each one of us. But we are pilgrims and wayfarers, walking a common road, called to support and strengthen each other as we together walk the path of lifelong discipleship.

Faith, Hope, and Love in the Path of Discipleship

When Lewis and Clark set out on their trek across the unmapped wilderness of the North American continent, they took great care to equip themselves for what was likely to come. They gathered all the knowledge they could find about the lands ahead, and they brought supplies and tools to get them well launched. But they knew that most of their provisions would be found on the way: food, water, shelter, and human guides. They had no clear maps of the area; they had to make judgments about the best course to take in uncharted territory.

In a similar way, when we set out on the path of discipleship, we want to count the cost and equip ourselves with everything we can in order to walk that path successfully. But most of what we will need lies ahead of us. We need to trust in God for our daily provision and place our hope in his providential grace if we are to persevere and reach our goal. There are many gifts and graces available to us as we walk the path of discipleship: the Scriptures, the sacraments, the gifts and fruits of the Spirit, and many more.

To conclude our study of discipleship, we would like to revisit the roles of the theological virtues—faith, hope, and love—in the life of a disciple. These primary gifts of grace provide us with crucial and essential resources for successfully living a joyful, adventurous life in Christ. First we will consider faith and hope, and then we will conclude by examining love of God and neighbor through the lens of friendship.

Faith

The *Catechism* states the core meaning of faith: "Faith is the theological virtue by which we believe in God and believe all that he has said and revealed to us, and that Holy Church proposes for our belief, because he is truth itself" (1814). But a full expression of faith also includes the commitment of our lives, as we entrust ourselves completely to God. "Faith is first of all a personal adherence of man to God. . . . It is right and just to entrust oneself wholly to God and to believe absolutely what he says" (*Catechism*, 150).

In one sense, faith is the door by which we enter into a relationship with God in Christ; faith comes at the beginning. But faith is also the gift of grace within us by which we continue to trust God and offer ourselves to him. We don't leave faith behind as we become mature disciples; rather, faith matures and continues to play an essential role in meeting the challenges and trials that we face.

In a landmark homily, St. John Henry Newman calls us to embrace the "ventures of faith" that are required of a Christian, not only at the beginning of life in Christ but across the entire journey as disciples. "Here then a great lesson is impressed upon us, that our duty as Christians lies in this, in making ventures for eternal life without the absolute certainty of success."[110] What does Newman mean by the phrase "ventures of faith"?

> This, indeed, is the very meaning of the word "venture"; for that is a strange venture which has nothing in it of fear, risk, danger, anxiety, uncertainty. Yes, so it certainly is; and in this consists the excellence and nobleness of *faith*; this is the very reason why *faith* is singled out from other graces, . . . because its presence implies that we have the heart to make a venture.[111]

There is nothing safe or predictable about this aspect of faith. On the one hand, this active, venturing faith is noble and generous. It is not fearful or constrained. On the other hand, it is not rash or frivolous but grounded in the faithfulness and providence of God. The faith-filled person is able to step out and risk everything for God, at each stage of life. Whether we are natural risk takers or naturally risk averse, we are *all* called to invest our lives in the kingdom of God with a venturesome faith.

> The faith-filled person is able to step out and risk everything for God, at each stage of life.

This is what Mary did when the angel announced to her a jarring and unexpected message. Yes, Mary received all the grace needed to fulfill her role in God's plan, but this does not mean that she was forewarned in detail about what God would ask of her, so that she was able to practice her part ahead of time. There was no prepared script for her to follow. The angel Gabriel appeared without forewarning, and when he greeted Mary, she "was greatly troubled . . . and considered in her mind what sort of greeting this might be" (Luke 1:29). Gabriel then announced God's plan, that Mary was to bear a son, the Messiah.

Mary's response came in the form of a question: "How can this be?" (Luke 1:34). Gabriel explained that it would occur through the power of the Spirit:

> The Holy Spirit will come upon you,
> and the power of the Most High will overshadow you;
> therefore the child to be born will be called holy,
> the Son of God. (1:35)

The drama here is intense. What will Mary do? How will she respond to this unexpected interruption in her life?

Showing herself to be the model disciple, Mary put her faith into action and replied, "Behold, I am the handmaid of the Lord; let it be to me according to your word" (Luke 1:38). In Mary's free, faith-filled response to the initiative of God, "Let it be to me according to your word," we see how a venturesome faith enables us to meet the call of God at each stage in our lives.

Hope

What role does hope play in helping us press on as disciples for the whole of our lives?

Hope is the virtue that provides a living connection to our heavenly destiny; it enables us to live *now* in the strength and encouragement that come from knowing we are bound for eternal life with God. The apostle Paul tells us that, as disciples, we live by hope: "Now hope that is seen is not hope. For who hopes for what he sees? But if we hope for what we do not see, we wait for it with patience" (Romans 8:24-25).

The *Catechism* describes hope in this way:

Hope is the theological virtue by which we desire the kingdom of heaven and eternal life as our happiness, placing our trust in Christ's promises and relying not on our own strength, but on the help of the grace of the Holy Spirit. (1817)

Through the activity of hope, we trust not in ourselves or what we see in the world, but in the promises of Christ.

The *Catechism* further describes what hope accomplishes in us as we journey through life: "[I]t keeps man from discouragement; it sustains him during times of abandonment; it opens up his heart in expectation of eternal beatitude" (1818). It is hope that bears us up and enables us to persevere through trials, hardships, perplexity, and setbacks.

> The true measure of our discipleship is how well we love.

We cannot know ahead of time what trials and crises we will encounter along the road, but we can be confident because of the hope that lives and acts within us. We have the biblical promise that God will give us the strength and perseverance to carry on in faithfulness:

No testing has overtaken you that is not common to everyone. God is faithful, and he will not let you be tested beyond your strength, but with the testing he will also provide the way out so that you may be able to endure it. (1 Corinthians 10:13; NRSVCE)

The hope we are talking about here is not certainty that everything in this life will turn out well; it is not an optimistic view of the world. Instead, hope assures us that we are known and loved by God and called to eternal life, and it produces in us joy and energy for living and acting in this world and seeing God's purposes come to pass. As we make our way as disciples, traversing the various crossroads along the way, supernatural hope provides a crucial help, not only to persevere but to flourish as joyful disciples of Christ.

Paradoxically, having our hope in eternal life actually makes us more hopeful for this world as well: "Supernatural hope, then . . . is able to rejuvenate and give new vigor even to natural hope."[112] Those of us who hope in Christ for eternal life should also have hope *for this life*, despite the insecurity and uncertainty of things in the world as we know it. As our hope in Christ deepens, our hope for the world also increases. It is precisely because the source of our hope is not *in* this world but *in* Christ that, as missionary disciples sent into the world, we can have hope *for* this world.

Love

In no uncertain terms, Jesus established the heart of missionary discipleship: we are called to love God with all our heart, soul, mind, and strength and to love one another as ourselves (see Matthew 22:34-40; Mark 12:28-34). These two commandments sum up the law and the prophets of the Old Testament. "God is love" (1 John 4:8, 16), and love will endure to eternal life (see 1 Corinthians 13:8, 13). Above everything else, we are called to clothe ourselves in love for one another (see Colossians 3:14).

Simply put, the true measure of our discipleship is how well we love. If we seek to cultivate a vision for lifelong discipleship, if our aim is to form mature disciples, then we must make love our aim (see 1 Corinthians 14:1) and seek to grow in charity (see 1 Thessalonians 3:12). If we fail in love, then our labors for the kingdom of God will not amount to much (see 1 Corinthians 13:1-3). And the greatest expression of love is laying down our lives for God (as martyrs) and for one another (as fellow servants and friends).

Friendship with One Another and with God

Friendship with One Another

In an age of hyper-individualism, when more and more people are living alone and fewer people are having children, we believe it is essential to form disciples who know what it means to live in committed communities of mutual friendship. Real friendship, grounded in Christ, is an important antidote to a world marked by superficial relationships and terminal loneliness. If we seek to raise up missionary disciples but fail to help these disciples form communities of friends, then something essential is lacking. If we hope to fulfill the command to love one another, then we need to be in real communities that call forth sacrificial love.

The First Letter of John teaches us that if we fail to love our brother or sister whom we see, then we cannot claim to love God, whom we cannot see (see 4:20). By building committed communities of friends—and forming others to do so—we not only learn what it means to love one another but also learn more deeply what it means to love God.

Friendship has become a very hot topic today—and rightly so. The TV sitcom *Friends*, one of the most widely watched TV series on record, portrayed a felt need to form a community of friends amid an increasingly rootless society. The drive to gather hundreds of friends on social media reflects a contemporary thirst for friendship—for belonging and identity. We live in a world deeply hungry, even desperate, for friendship, but real friendship remains in short supply.

The plight of same-sex attracted people should cause us all to think more deeply about the importance of friendship. In a culture that glorifies sex and considers sexual expression essential to personal happiness, many argue that it is unfair and unreasonable to ask same-sex attracted people to refrain from sexual activity. The underlying assumption is that true human happiness requires a sexual partner of one's own choosing. This is assumed to be a basic human right.

To counter this view, many same-sex attracted Christians have spoken out with great courage about their commitment to follow Christ's teaching on sexuality and so refrain from same-sex activity. But they also describe the loneliness and isolation they often experience, even within the Church. Their situation has put the spotlight on the need to rejuvenate a vision for non-erotic friendships that bring life and fulfillment—and this need is not only for same-sex attracted people but for *all* Christians.

Friendship is a gift of God to his people. Consequently, to communicate the nature of true friendship in Christ, to gain wisdom about how to form such friendships, and to enkindle enthusiasm for building committed communities where friendship in Christ will be valued and cultivated are critical pastoral priorities for today.

Christian discipleship thrives in a *communal* context. We are not lone Christians walking a solitary pilgrimage of faith. Rather we are banded together with other companions in a common pilgrimage—serving together, standing together against a common foe, and helping each other thrive along the way.

Crucially, our friendships in Christ are not merely instrumental, not just things that help us make progress on the path. The goal of eternal life is communion (*koinonia*) with God and with one another. Our friendships here in this life are the training ground and foretaste of the friendships that will be ours eternally. Christian discipleship, at its core, is also a school of friendship.

But the casual, informal model of friendship on offer today simply won't provide what we need. When personal compatibility and common interest alone provide the grounds for friendship, we are building on shifting sands that won't weather the storms that will come. Even within marriage, committed love provides the primary anchor for the development of friendship between the spouses, not the other way around. If friendship is to flourish, then we need to cultivate committed communities of disciples who gather, not primarily in fact for friendship, but to love and serve God and advance the mission of the gospel.

In such settings, friendships can develop easily and naturally. In this "missional" context, a wide variety of friendships can flourish—some stronger, some more modest—without the intense pressure that often accompanies gatherings of people who are primarily seeking friendship as their goal. Families will naturally be the bedrock of these committed communities, but ample space should be made for singles, young and old, who are full members, not second-class citizens of the Christian community.

We might ask ourselves: "Who are the people that I am called to befriend? Who are the people God has placed in my life to be friends for the journey, gifts from his hand? And how can I nourish these friendships and recognize the great gifts that they are?"

Christ—who has called us to be his friends—is our model and guide. And the Holy Spirit is the person (and power) living within us who teaches and directs us in forming friendships that reflect and participate in the Trinitarian communion of love.

Friendship with God

In the pursuit of lifelong discipleship, cultivating love for God is paramount. The Catholic tradition possesses tremendous riches, far more than we can speak about here, to help disciples on the pilgrimage grow in the love of God. We wish to draw attention to one important expression of our love for God: namely, becoming friends of God and growing in this friendship over time.

The idea of being a friend of God finds its roots in the Old Testament. Moses is marked out as the particular friend of God because of his intimacy with the Lord (see Exodus

33:11), and the Letter of James tells us that Abraham was also a "friend of God" (2:23). Psalm 25:14 says, "The friendship of the LORD is for those who fear him," while the Book of Wisdom declares that divine wisdom finds a home in holy people and causes them to become God's friends (see 7:27).

In the New Testament, we become friends of God by becoming friends of Christ. John the Baptist identifies himself as the "friend of the bridegroom" (John 3:29) who gladly steps aside so that the bride (that is, the Church) may be joined to her true bridegroom (that is, Christ).

Our invitation to become Christ's friends comes from Jesus himself. He invites his intimate disciples to consider themselves no longer just servants but genuine friends of the master:

> You are my friends if you do what I command you. No longer do I call you servants, for the servant does not know what his master is doing; but I have called you friends, for all that I have heard from my Father I have made known to you. (John 15:14-15)

This is a remarkable invitation! The disciples of Jesus, who listen to his voice and obey his word, are raised up to be his friends. Jesus brings his tested disciples into the intimacy of friendship.

How does this friendship come to pass? Primarily through the gift of the indwelling Spirit. Jesus promises the disciples, "And I will pray the Father, and he will give you another Counselor, to be with you for ever, even the Spirit of truth. . . . You know him, for he dwells with you, and will be in you" (John 14:16-17). The intimate friendship that we have with God comes about through the dwelling of the Trinity—Father, Son, and Spirit—in the soul of the believer.

In our day, the topic of friendship with God has received new emphasis. In his inaugural homily as pope, Benedict XVI praised the beauty of friendship with Christ with these words:

> Only in this friendship are the doors of life opened wide. Only in this friendship is the great potential of human existence truly revealed. Only in this friendship do we experience beauty and liberation.[113]

Pope Francis likewise identifies friendship with God as the mature expression of our encounter with the love of God:

> Thanks solely to this encounter—or renewed encounter—with God's love, which blossoms into an enriching friendship, we are liberated from our narrowness and self-absorption. We become fully human when we become more than human, when we let God bring us beyond ourselves in order to attain the fullest truth of our being. Here we find the source and inspiration of all our efforts at evangelization.[114]

When we encounter the living God, we encounter his love, and this love is meant to grow into a mature and reciprocal friendship. From this friendship comes a renewed motivation to bring the good news of Jesus to others.

The longtime preacher of the papal household, Fr. Raniero Cantalamessa, invites us to consider the greatness of the friendship that Christ extends to each of us. He observes that Christians often miss the invitation to be a friend of

Christ: "Unfortunately, Jesus is rarely thought of as a friend and confidant."

Why is this so? Because we tend to treat him as risen, ascended, and now no longer really accessible in this intimate way:

> We forget that being "true man," as the dogma says—and even being the very perfection of humanity itself—he possesses the capacity for friendship to the highest degree, which is one of the noblest characteristics of a human being. It is Jesus who wants that relationship with us. . . .
>
> During his earthly life, . . . it is only with some . . . that Jesus has a relationship of true friendship. Now that he is risen and is no longer subject to the limitations of the body, . . . he offers every man and woman the possibility of having him as a friend in the fullest sense of that word.[115]

Friendship with God in Christ will look different for each of us, but we can expect the following qualities to be part of our experience of divine friendship:

First, friendship with Jesus Christ means that we know and encounter him personally—and continue to do so. This encounter may have a strong emotional quality, but this is not necessary or essential to genuine friendship.

Second, friendship with Jesus Christ means that we relate to him as a companion, one who is side-by-side with us. God in Christ has come down to us, taken on our nature, and spoken to us in our language. And he continues to do this with his friends. To be a friend of Jesus is to know that he is within us and that he dwells among us.

Third, friendship with Jesus Christ means that we know his love for us and that we are ready to lay down our lives for him and for our fellow disciples. Friends don't just speak to each other; they love each other. And the primary way that Jesus loved us is that he laid down his life for us, his friends (see John 15:13).

Jesus called people to become his disciples. And he called his disciples to "make disciples" of others (Matthew 28:19). This call to discipleship is a call to Christian maturity. Our hope is that this book will help—even in a small way—inspire, inform, and equip the Church to carry out the noble work of forming mature disciples. And our prayer is that the "Lord of the harvest" will send many more laborers to bring the good news of the kingdom to the world (9:38).

Notes

1. Pope Francis, *Evangelii Gaudium* [On the Proclamation of the Gospel in Today's World], November 24, 2013, 24, https://www.vatican.va/content/francesco/en/apost_exhortations/documents/papa-francesco_esortazione-ap_20131124_evangelii-gaudium.html.
2. George Weigel, *Evangelical Catholicism: Deep Reform in the 21st-Century Church* (New York: Basic Books, 2013), 36.
3. Weigel, 82.
4. Sherry Weddell, *Forming Intentional Disciples: The Path to Knowing and Following Jesus* (Huntington, IN: Our Sunday Visitor, 2012).
5. Curtis Martin, *Making Missionary Disciples: How to Live the Method Modeled by the Master* (Genesee, CO: FOCUS, 2018).
6. For other excellent recent descriptions of what it means to become disciples of Christ, see Edward Sri, *Into His Likeness: Be Transformed as a Disciple of Christ* (Greenwood Village, CO: Augustine Institute, 2017), and Jeff Cavins, *The Activated Disciple: Taking Your Faith to the Next Level* (West Chester, PA: Ascension Press, 2018).
7. The mission statement of St. Paul's Outreach (SPO) is "to build transformational communities that form missionary disciples for life." For more information, go to https://spo.org/.
8. University Christian Outreach (UCO) identifies "discipleship" as one of its core elements: "UCO equips students to become lifelong disciples of Jesus Christ by following his teaching and responding to his calling in family, career, church, and mission." For more information, go to http://ucoweb.org/.
9. Vatican II, *Gaudium et Spes* [Pastoral Constitution on the Church in the Modern World], December 7, 1965, 3-4, http://www.vatican.va/archive/hist_councils/ii_vatican_council/documents/vat-ii_cons_19651207_gaudium-et-spes_en.html.
10. *Gaudium et Spes*, 4.

11. Pope John Paul II, *Christifideles Laici* [Apostolic Exhortation on the Vocation and the Mission of the Lay Faithful in the Church and in the World], December 30, 1988, 3, http://w2.vatican.va/content/john -paul-ii/en/apost_exhortations/documents/hf_jp-ii_exh_30121988 _christifideles-laici.html.

12. See Pew Research Center, "In US, Decline of Christianity Continues at Rapid Pace," October 17, 2019, https://www.pewforum.org/2019/10/17/ in-u-s-decline-of-christianity-continues-at-rapid-pace/.

13. Pope Benedict XVI, *Porta Fidei*, Apostolic Letter for the Indiction of the Year of Faith, October 11, 2011, 2, http://w2.vatican.va/content/ benedict-xvi/en/motu_proprio/documents/hf_ben-xvi_motu -proprio_20111011_porta-fidei.html.

14. *Christifideles Laici*, 34.

15. See Alexander Solzhenitsyn, Templeton Address 1983, as adapted by *National Review*, December 11, 2018, https://www.nationalreview .com/2018/12/aleksandr-solzhenitsyn-men-have-forgotten-god-speech/.

16. *Christifideles Laici*, 34.

17. *Laudato Si'* [Encyclical Letter on the Care for Our Common Home], May 24, 2015, 22, http://w2.vatican.va/content/francesco/en/encyclicals/ documents/papa-francesco_20150524_enciclica-laudato-si.html.

18. Brian Starks and Maureen Day, *National Study on Catholic Campus Ministry*, preparation materials, 2018, United States Conference of Catholic Bishops, Washington, DC. Used with permission.

19. Weddell, 39.

20. J. R. R. Tolkien, *The Fellowship of the Ring* (New York: Ballantine Books, 1965), 76.

21. Cardinal Joseph Ratzinger and Vittorio Messori, *The Ratzinger Report: An Exclusive Interview on the State of the Church* (San Francisco: Ignatius Press, 1985), 153.

22. Pope John Paul II, *Redemptoris Missio* [Encyclical on the Church's Missionary Mandate], December 7 1990, 2, 86, http://www.vatican.va/ content/john-paul-ii/en/encyclicals/documents/hf_jp-ii_enc_07121990 _redemptoris-missio.html.

23. George Weigel, "The Rise of Evangelical Catholicism," *First Things*, February 6, 2013, https://www.firstthings.com/web-exclusives/2013/02/ the-rise-of-evangelical-catholicism.

24. *Evangelii Gaudium*, 33.

25. *Evangelii Gaudium* 33.

26. Pope John Paul II, *Tertio Millennio Adveniente* [On Preparation for the Jubilee of the Year 2000], November 10, 1994, 44, https://w2.vatican .va/content/john-paul-ii/en/apost_letters/1994/documents/hf_jp-ii _apl_19941110_tertio-millennio-adveniente.html.

27. Pope Paul VI, *Evangelii Nuntiandi* [Evangelization in the Modern World], December 8, 1975, 14, http://w2.vatican.va/content/paul-vi/en/apost_exhortations/documents/hf_p-vi_exh_19751208_evangelii-nuntiandi.html.

28. *Redemptoris Missio*, 3.

29. Archbishop Salvatore Fisichella, "We Need New Evangelizers" (Sydney, Australia, Aug. 9, 2012), http://www.annusfidei.va/content/novaevangelizatio/en/news/09-08-2012.html.

30. *General Directory for Catechesis*, 58, cited in Pope John Paul II, *Redemptoris Missio*, 33.

31. *Evangelii Gaudium*, 25, quoting Fifth General Conference of the Latin American and Caribbean Bishops, *Aparecida Document*, June 29, 2007, 201.

32. Pope John Paul II, Address to the Meeting with Ecclesial Movements and New Communities, May 30, 1998, 7, http://w2.vatican.va/content/john-paul-ii/en/speeches/1998/may/documents/hf_jp-ii_spe_19980530_riflessioni.html.

33. *Gaudium et Spes*, 24.

34. Cardinal Joseph Ratzinger, Address to Catechists and Religion Teachers, December 2000, Introduction, https://d2y1pz2y630308.cloudfront.net/5032/documents/2014/0/ADDRESS%20TO%20CATECHISTS%20AND%20RELIGION%20TEACHERS.pdf.

35. Pope John Paul II, *Novo Millennio Ineunte* [At the Close of the Great Jubilee of the Year 2000], January 6, 2001, 58, http://www.vatican.va/content/john-paul-ii/en/apost_letters/2001/documents/hf_jp-ii_apl_20010106_novo-millennio-ineunte.html.

36. For an insightful description of the common stages, or thresholds, in the process of conversion, see Sherry A. Weddell, *Forming Intentional Disciples: The Path to Knowing and Following Jesus*, 125-84.

37. Pope Benedict XVI, *Deus Caritas Est* [God Is Love], 1, vatican.va/content/benedict-xvi/en/encyclicals/documents/hf_ben-xvi_enc_20051225_deus-caritas-est.html.

38. *Into His Likeness: Be Transformed as a Disciple of Christ*, 23, 30.

39. Pope Benedict XVI, Letter to Seminarians, October 18, 2010, Introduction, http://www.vatican.va/content/benedict-xvi/en/letters/2010/documents/hf_ben-xvi_let_20101018_seminaristi.html.

40. *Evangelii Gaudium*, 120.

41. Among the more influential studies of Jesus' strategy of working intensely with small groups, see Robert E. Coleman, *The Master Plan of Evangelism* (Grand Rapids, MI: Revell Books, 1993), and Greg Ogden, *Transforming Discipleship: Making Disciples a Few at a Time* (Downers Grove, IL: InterVarsity Press, 2016).

42. Message of the Holy Father for the 48th World Day of Prayer for Vocations, May 15, 2011, http://www.vatican.va/content/benedict-xvi/en/messages/vocations/documents/hf_ben-xvi_mes_20101115_xlviii-vocations.html.

43. Dietrich von Hildebrand, *Transformation in Christ: On the Christian Attitude* (Manchester, NH: Sophia Institute Press, 1990), 9.

44. *Evangelii Gaudium*, 24.

45. *Evangelii Gaudium*, 160.

46. Weigel, 36.

47. Tom Bergler, *From Here to Maturity: Overcoming the Juvenilization of American Christianity* (Grand Rapids, MI: Eerdmans Publishing, 2014), 48.

48. Cardinal Joseph Ratzinger (Pope Benedict XVI), Address to Catechists and Religion Teachers, December 2000, 1, https://d2y1pz2y630308.cloudfront.net/5032/documents/2014/0/ADDRESS%20TO%20CATECHISTS%20AND%20RELIGION%20TEACHERS.pdf.

49. *Evangelii Gaudium*, 24.

50. *Gaudium et Spes*, 4.

51. *Christifideles Laici*, 32; emphasis in original.

52. See, for example, 2 Samuel 23:1-2; Luke 1:67-68; 2:27-28; Acts 4; 11:15-18.

53. *Evangelii Nuntiandi*, 75.

54. *Evangelii Nuntiandi*, 75.

55. *Evangelii Nuntiandi*, 27, citing cf. Ephesians 2:8; Romans 1:16. Cf. Sacred Congregation for the Doctrine of the Faith, *Declaratio ad fidem tuendam in mysteria Incarnationis et SS. Trinitatis e quibusdam recentibus erroribus* (February 21,1972): *Acta Apostolicae Sedis*, 64 (1972), 237-241..

56. *Evangelii Nuntiandi*, 4.

57. *The Apostolic Tradition of Hippolytus*, as cited in Kenan Osborne, *The Christian Sacraments of Initiaition: Baptism, Confirmation, Eucharist* (New York: Paulist Press, 1987), 65.

58. *Didascalia Apostolorum*, quoted in Paul Bradshaw, *Reconstructing Early Christian Worship* (London, UK: Society for Promoting Christian Knowledge, 2012)._

59. Osborne, 65.

60. The *Didache*, as cited in D. H. Williams, *Origins of Christian Tradition* (Grand Rapids, MI: Baker Publishing Group, 2006), 45.

61. Osborne, 15.6–7.

62. Osborne, 20.1.

63. Pope Francis, Christmas Address, December 21, 2019, https://www
.vatican.va/content/francesco/it/speeches/2019/december/documents/
papa-francesco_20191221_curia-romana
.html.

64. Raniero Cantalamessa, "The Year of Faith and the *Catechism of the Catholic Church*," First Advent Sermon, December 7, 2012, http://www
.cantalamessa.org/?p=1876&lang=en.

65. Pope Francis, Address to the Roman Curia, December 21, 2019, citing
his 2013 interview with Fr. Antonio Spadaro, http://w2.vatican
.va/content/francesco/en/speeches/2019/december/documents/papa
-francesco_20191221_curia-romana.html.

66. *Evangelii Gaudium*, 15, citing Fifth General Conference of the Latin
American and Caribbean Bishops, *Aparecida Document*, June 29, 2007,
548, 370..

67. *Evangelii Nuntiandi*, 46.

68. Mother Teresa, *A Simple Path* (New York: Ballantyne Books, 1995),
quoted at https://www.goodreads.com/quotes/139677-the-greatest
-disease-in-the-west-today-is-not-tb.

69. Raniero Cantalamessa, Fourth Advent Homily, section 2, December 23,
2011, https://zenit.org/articles/father-cantalamessa-s-4th-advent
-sermon-2/.

70. *Christifidelis Laici*, 57; emphasis in original.

71. *Christifidelis Laici*, 58.

72. *Christifidelis Laici*, 58; emphasis in original.

73. See *Gaudium et Spes*, 43.

74. One potential criticism of this form of common prayer is that it might
detract from the liturgy of the Eucharist: people might find this prayer
more appealing or exciting and so lose their taste for—and appreciation
of—"the source and summit" of our life with God in the Eucharist
(*Catechism*, 1324). Our experience is just the opposite. When people
learn how to approach God personally in prayer—when prayer comes
alive for them—the liturgy and the sacraments take on a new and more
powerful role. Common prayer, rightly configured, draws its strength
and power from the liturgy of the Eucharist and in turn enhances the
role of the Eucharist in our lives.

75. For excellent sociological studies of the religious habits and beliefs of
young people, see Christian Smith and Melinda Lundquist Denton, *Soul
Searching: The Religious and Spiritual Lives of American Teenagers*
(New York: Oxford University Press, 2005); Christian Smith with
Patricia Snell, *Souls in Transition: The Religious and Spiritual Lives of
Emerging Adults* (New York: Oxford University Press, 2009); Christian
Smith with Kari Christoffersen, Hilary Davidson, and Patricia Snell

Herzog, *Lost in Transition: The Dark Side of Emerging Adulthood* (New York: Oxford University Press, 2011); and Christian Smith with Kyle Longest, Jonathan Hill, and Kari Christoffersen, *Young Catholic America: Emerging Adults In, Out of, and Gone from the Church* (New York: Oxford University Press, 2014).

76. *Evangelii Gaudium*, 173.
77. *Evangelii Gaudium*, 120.
78. *Evangelii Gaudium*, 120.
79. Martin, 4; emphasis in original.
80. In our student work, we have two courses that contribute directly to cultivating this common community environment. The first is Christian Personal Relations, which lays out biblical patterns of relating together; the second is The Fruit of the Spirit, which describes the character qualities that disciples of Christ are meant to cultivate through the Spirit.
81. *Christifidelis Laici*, 58.
82. *Christifidelis Laici*, 16.
83. Pope John Paul II, *Ubi et Orbi* Message, December 25, 1978, 1, http://www.vatican.va/content/john-paul-ii/en/messages/urbi/documents/hf_jp-ii_mes_19781225_urbi.html.
84. The Pontifical Council for the Family, *The Truth and Meaning of Human Sexuality*, December 8, 1995, 1, http://www.vatican.va/roman_curia/pontifical_councils/family/documents/rc_pc_family_doc_08121995_human-sexuality-en.html.
85. Pope John Paul II, *Evangelium Vitae* [On the Value and Inviolability of Human Life], March 25, 1995, 12, 19, and elsewhere, http://www.vatican.va/content/john-paul-ii/en/encyclicals/documents/hf_jp-ii_enc_25031995_evangelium-vitae.html.
86. *Novo Millennio Ineunte*, 32.
87. We recommend Thomas Dubay, SM, *Prayer Primer: Igniting a Fire Within* (Cincinnati, OH: Servant, 2002); and Peter Kreeft, *Prayer for Beginners* (San Francisco: Ignatius, 2009).
88. "The divine image is present in every man. It shines forth in the communion of persons, in the likeness of the union of the divine persons among themselves" (*Catechism*, 1702).
89. Ralph Waldo Emerson, as cited in Andy Deane, *Learn to Study the Bible* (Maitland, FL: Xulon Press, 2009), 35.
90. Vatican II, *Unitatis Redintegratio* [On Ecumenism], November 21, 1964, 11, https://www.vatican.va/archive/hist_councils/ii_vatican_council/documents/vat-ii_decree_19641121_unitatis-redintegratio_en.html.
91. *Evangelium Vitae*, 54.

92. For short helpful definitions of the cardinal virtues, see *Catechism*, 1806–09.

93. For short helpful definitions of the theological virtues, see *Catechism*, 1814, 1817, 1822.

94. *Suscipe* of St. Ignatius Loyola.

95. *Christifideles Laici*, 58; emphasis in original.

96. *Evangelii Gaudium*, 10, citing *Aparecida Document*, 360.

97. *Evangelii Nuntiandi*, 24.

98. *Evangelii Gaudium*, 2.

99. *Evangelii Nuntiandi*, 14.

100. *Lumen Gentium*, 31.

101. *Christifideles Laici*, 34; emphasis in original.

102. *Evangelii Gaudium*, 24. George Weigel, in *Evangelical Catholicism: Deep Reform in the 21st-Century Church*, 36, calls for a "mission-centered community of disciples with a clear sense of identity and purpose."

103. *Christifideles Laici*, 20; emphasis added.

104. *Evangelii Gaudium*, 49.

105. *Evangelii Nuntiandi*, 15.

106. *Evangelii Nuntiandi*, 41.

107. *Evangelii Gaudium*, 150.

108. The vehicle we have used most commonly is The Life in the Spirit Seminars (LSS). We have reworked the LSS for students into a weekend format that we call "Fan into Flame." The Alpha Course provides a similar format for presenting the basic gospel message and inviting people to respond in faith and encounter the living Christ through the Spirit.

109. For an elaboration of the gospel as the true adventure of the world, see Daniel A. Keating, *The Adventure of Discipleship* (Steubenville, OH: Emmaus Road Publishing, 2018).

110. Cardinal John Henry Newman, "The Ventures of Faith," in *Parochial and Plain Sermons* (San Francisco: Ignatius Press, 1997), 922.

111. Newman, 914; emphasis in original.

112. Josef Pieper, *Faith, Hope, Love* (San Francisco: Ignatius Press, 1986), 109–110.

113. Pope Benedict XVI, Homily of His Holiness Benedict XVI for the Inauguration of His Pontificate, April 24, 2005, http://www.vatican .va/content/benedict-xvi/en/homilies/2005/documents/hf_ben-xvi _hom_20050424_inizio-pontificato.html.

114. *Evangelii Gaudium*, 8.

115. Fr. Raniero Cantalamessa, Fourth Lenten Homily, April 4, 2014, 4, https://zenit.org/articles/father-cantalamessa-s-4th-lent-homily-2014.

About the Authors

Gordon DeMarais is the founder and president of Saint Paul's Outreach. He has been actively involved with the teaching, formation, and evangelization of university students and young adults in the Twin Cities area and around the country for over thirty years. Gordy and his wife, Teresa, have six children and six grandchildren. They live in Inver Grove Heights, Minnesota.

Dr. Daniel Keating is Professor of Theology at Sacred Heart Major Seminary, where he teaches on Scripture, the Church Fathers, Ecumenism, and the New Evangelization. He served as a theological consultant for the doctrine committee of the United States Catholic Bishop's Conference (USCCB), and is a Catholic participant in the national Catholic-Evangelical dialogue. Dr. Keating lives in Ann Arbor, Michigan, where he is a member of the Servants of the Word, a lay brotherhood dedicated to the work of evangelization and Christian unity.